THE
NATURAL
DOG

**FOR DAN, WHO BRINGS
LOVE AND STRENGTH,
AND TO VIZSLA OTTO
WHO SHARES HIS
CRAZY JOY WITH US**

First published in Great Britain in 2021
by Hamlyn, an imprint of
Octopus Publishing Group Ltd
Carmelite House
50 Victoria Embankment
London EC4Y 0DZ
www.octopusbooks.co.uk

An Hachette UK Company
www.hachette.co.uk

Distributed in the US by
Hachette Book Group
1290 Avenue of the Americas
4th and 5th Floors
New York, NY 10104

Distributed in Canada by
Canadian Manda Group
664 Annette St.
Toronto, Ontario, Canada M6S 2C8

ISBN 978-0-600-63603-8

A CIP catalogue record for this book is
available from the British Library.

Printed and bound in China

10 9 8 7 6 5 4 3 2 1

Publishing Director: Trevor Davies
Senior Editors: Pollyanna Poulter and
        Pauline Bache
Senior Designer: Jaz Bahra
Picture Library Manager: Jennifer Veall
Production Controller: Serena Savini
Copy Editor: Sam Stanley
Proofreader: Jo Smith
Indexer: Isobel McLean

THE
NATURAL
DOG

A new approach to achieving
a happy, healthy hound

GWEN BAILEY

hamlyn

CONTENTS

Part 2 – The Mentally Happy Dog

INTRODUCTION

The concept of wellness – actively making choices and being aware of the consequences of those choices in order to work towards optimal health and wellbeing – is new and powerful. It is a process only recently focused on by modern humans, although its roots can be traced back to ancient civilizations. *The Natural Dog* looks at how you can achieve this for your dog. It will help you give your dog the best quality of life and the longest life possible.

Wellness is not a passive state but, instead, more of an active pursuit where intentions, choices and actions work towards an optimal state of health and wellbeing. As a result of small changes, your dog can gradually become naturally calmer, healthier and happier.

To truly embrace the wellness culture, you need to consider fitness and fulfillment, both of the mind and body. This book will look at optimum nutrition for your canine friend, as well as how to provide all the physical and mental exercise needed to live well. Thorny subjects such as preventative medicine and the pros and cons of neutering are tackled with a focus on your dog's wellbeing.

It will show you how to develop an incredible relationship where your dog trusts you unreservedly, leading to confidence, fun and a reduction of stress levels, which, in turn, leads to better behaviour, lower vet fees and a happier and longer life. The information presented here is what dogs would want you to know if they could talk.

The Natural Dog contains a distillation of all the information I have acquired over a lifetime of helping people in a professional capacity with their problem dogs, from great teachers and fellow professionals via all the hours of continuing professional development I've attended over the years, as well as the knowledge gained from owning dogs all my life and being intensely interested in all aspects of their care. There is now so much to learn about dogs from books and courses and I have put the most important information together for you and included all those bits of knowledge that so many owners get into trouble from not knowing. The content is designed to fill gaps that exist for many owners.

This book could not have been written without the expert help and knowledge of the wonderful holistic veterinary surgeon Nick Thompson BSc (Vet Sci) Hons, BVM&S, VetMFHom, MRCVS. Nick is someone who puts the welfare of animals first and foremost and is not afraid to think outside

the box to put new ideas and research into practice that make an immediate and immense difference to their lives. Nick gave me the confidence and the extra knowledge I needed to write the first part of this book which could, and should, have only been written in conjunction with a veterinary professional, and I am extremely grateful for all I have learned from him that I am now able to pass on to you.

Throughout this book I have used the term 'owner' rather than 'guardian'. While 'owner' will eventually be an old-fashioned term, with all its connotations, and certainly does not do the relationship we have with our dogs justice, we are not there yet and the term 'guardian' is still somewhat unknown. Hence I have used 'owner' in this book to avoid any confusion to the reader.

My hope is that, as a result of reading *The Natural Dog*, you will be able to improve the quality of your dog's life in realistic and sustainable ways that will pay real dividends for their happiness and welfare. By taking a holistic view of your dog's wellbeing, you can improve life for your best friend, ensuring your dog lives in an optimal way that will bring the added bonus of a longer and happier time together.

PART 1

THE PHYSICALLY HEALTHY DOG

CHAPTER 1

Physical exercise

My newly adopted Labrador/Weimaraner cross had been cooped up in kennels for nearly a year waiting for a home.

On his first walk, I let him and my other dogs off lead in safe fields next to a river and he ran flat out for 1½ hours, stopping only to decide which new direction he should take. It was lovely to watch him relish that delicious feeling of freedom and he returned with us to the car with eyes glowing, tongue nearly to the floor and sides heaving. He wasn't fit, having spent most of the past year slowly padding around a small pen, but at 18 months he had enough energy and stamina to run for over an hour. The next day, without showing any signs of stiffness, we walked and he ran for another 1½ hours, and the same thing happened the day after, although he was slowing a little. By the end of the week he had settled down to a more normal behaviour pattern similar to my other young dogs, running sometimes but spending a lot of time sniffing and exploring, as if the threat of never being free to run again had faded from his mind.

Exercise is essential to wellbeing, and it's one of the first things to tackle when considering how to make adjustments for your dog's optimal state of living. The right amount of physical exercise can help your dog to feel happy and contented, as well as bringing important health benefits, and is an important element in the pursuit of wellness.

Couch potato or canine athlete?

When it comes to physical exercise, all dogs are different. Some love their home comforts and refuse walks unless conditions are perfect, and some, like my Hungarian Vizsla, will happily work and play energetically outside all day, every day. Exercise requirements will also depend on age and fitness levels. Owners, too, have different exercise tastes and when there is a mismatch between how much exercising you want to do and what your dog needs, problems and frustrations will inevitably arise.

Our pet dogs are usually chosen on looks alone, but behind each body type are years of selective breeding. Whether purebred or crossbred, the genetic make-up of your dog will impart certain traits and propensities and the desire to exercise will be one of them. Some dogs, including many of the dogs bred originally to be gun dogs or the herding breeds, such as Springer Spaniels and German Shepherds, will be descended from dogs bred to have the stamina to be physically and mentally active all day. Others, such as many of the toy breeds like Pekingese, will be from generations of pet dogs, whose only task was to sleep and be sociable. Some dogs, sadly, have such compromised bodies and breathing apparatus that they never feel like running far and will amble slowly at walking pace or sometimes not want to walk at all if it's too hot or conditions are less than ideal.

It is a good idea to research your dog's genetic make-up, through DNA testing if necessary, to find out what breeds are present and the jobs those breeds were bred for and take a good look at your dog's body shape. Comparing it to a wild dog or wolf body shape can help you predict how much energy and desire to exercise your dog will have.

How much is enough?

Balancing how much your dog wants to exercise with how much time you have to take them out is essential if you want your dog to be happy and healthy. Although this is not always easy, especially if you work all day and come home tired to a dog who is ready to burn off all their surplus energy, it is important to provide sufficient outlets for their physical and mental energy (see page 190).

If you don't do this, life with an under-exercised dog can be challenging. Quite apart from it being frustrating for the dog, there will be consequences for the owner. For an energetic animal with a zest for life, living with humans who only venture outside for short periods, who sit and watch screens for hours on end, and who have no interest in playing or walking must be maddening. All the dog's energy has to go somewhere. Dogs with too much unspent energy can be disruptive, noisy, boisterous, bad mannered and destructive.

Ask yourself – is your dog nicer to live with on a Sunday evening after a busy weekend? Or after a holiday with you when there were lots of opportunities to exercise? If so, and if problems start to build up during the week when they have too much time alone at home, you will know that you are not using enough of your dog's natural energy. Taking steps to rectify this will lead to a calmer, more contented dog that is easier to live with, to teach and enjoy.

Apart from the lack of fitness caused by a sedentary lifestyle, the stress caused by the frustration of having to remain still for long periods when their bodies would rather be on the move can lead to a weakened immune system and an increased risk of disease. Finding a way to routinely provide enough physical exercise for your dog, even if you have to buy in the services of a dog walker, can help you both to feel more contented and problem-free.

Conversely, there are some dogs, particularly small dogs or those with bodies that do not function very well, who do not want or need as much exercise as their owners might like. And some dogs are fearful about going outside and would rather stay at home. If there is a mismatch in this way, leaving your dog at home more often when you would rather take them out may be the compromise you have to make.

How much exercise to give is sometimes difficult to quantify and will depend on lots of factors, such as their genetic make-up, fitness level, age and state of health. A moderate amount of steady exercise all day is preferable to bursts of high activity just once or twice a day, but this is not always achievable for most owners. Too much exercise can result in a dog with aching limbs that is reluctant to walk, but too little exercise can lead to behaviour issues as your dog attempts to burn off excess energy. The best guide to 'how much' is the behaviour of your dog, both at home and on walks, rather than sticking rigidly to arbitrary guidelines. If your dog is lethargic and reluctant to exercise, do less (although if this is sudden in onset, a visit to the vet is important). If your dog is always bouncing and too boisterous, then more exercise is required, both physical and mental (see Part 2, Chapter 6).

Exercise patterns

Different types of dogs will prefer to exercise in different ways but looking at what your dog's ancestors were bred to do can help you work out how they will want to exercise. For example, sight hounds such as Greyhounds, Salukis and Afghan Hounds were bred for a high-speed chase over short distances, consequently they tend to exercise in short bursts of incredible speed and will be happy to walk beside you for the rest of the walk. Beagles and other hounds prefer a fast, continuous trot along strong scent trails left by prey animals and will often leave you on a walk to pursue their own fun at a faster speed. Dogs whose ancestors were bred to herd or be gundogs, such as Labrador Retrievers, will often prefer exercise that involves games and involvement with other dogs or the owner. Some dogs, such as smaller toy dogs, may find exercise less interesting and so will be content to stay beside you or even want to be carried if the walk is too long for them.

Finding out how your dog prefers to exercise and providing outlets that are acceptable and easy for you is the secret to a harmonious existence where both your and your dog's needs are met, whether that is safe free-running in dense vegetation for scent hounds or open grassy areas for sight hounds, providing activities on walks for herders or gundogs, or easy walks for smaller dogs.

Exercise solutions

It is important to find an exercise system that works for you and your dog. Try to find a range of options that fit into your daily life and arrange for all members of the family to join in so they can reap the benefits of exercise, share more dog time and take some of the responsibility for this essential part of dog ownership.

FREE RUNNING

The best type of exercise for any dog is being free to run and explore somewhere in a natural and varied environment. In such a place, dogs are free to expend as much energy as they like and to stop and rest when tired. It is by far the best type of exercise for all dogs, especially young puppies whose bones and joints are still developing and who can be harmed by long walks on the lead. For those owners who have limited time, free running is also cost effective in terms of time since it allows an energetic dog to use up energy fast without waiting for their slower human to travel the same distance. It can be hard to find wild places away from traffic and livestock where dogs can be safely off lead, so owning a dog that travels easily and that can be recalled if let off the lead will expand the number of areas where you can take your dog for free running.

A well-trained dog that has a really good recall can be safely let off lead in more places than one that runs off or stays, maddeningly, just out of reach, when you want to put the lead back on. A good dog trainer who can teach you how to get a successful and reliable recall with your dog, and one who uses only positive methods, is important. There are many more positive trainers than there used to be, so find one who understands the importance of proofing against distractions and calling over long distances as well as teaching the basic recall cue. Working with your dog to ensure your recall works is important if you want to have full control in all situations and it takes time and effort, as well as the correct knowledge and advice from your mentor. If your trainer is unable to get their dog to return when it is chasing a toy, or recommends using aversive or punishment-based methods, look elsewhere for help.

The secret to successful recalls is to have very high value 'wages' that your dog will be willing to leave what he is doing for, whether that is enjoying running free, sniffing interesting smells, playing with other dogs or even chasing. Most dogs only consider meat or treats with a very high meat content as high value so don't expect to get good results if you are 'paying' with a cereal-based treat. During adolescence or if your dog is really interested in its surroundings, food may not be a high enough reward for coming back to you. Teaching your dog to play with toys outside of the house and engaging more with them on walks will make your recalls more successful (see page 26).

While your dog is learning, one option is to find enclosed fields where they can run free safely. These may be hard to find, particularly if you live in a city, and they may require a considerable journey. Some dog trainers will have such fields available or there may be dog-safe fenced fields in your area that are offered commercially so it is worth checking the internet. Even hiring a fenced tennis court area may be suitable for training purposes. Such places provide complete peace of mind when walking an untrained dog and both of you can relax while you work on the training principles and games that will, one day, lead you to a less restricted life.

JOGGING OR CYCLING WITH YOUR DOG

Running or cycling with your dog attached to you or the bike requires training and the correct equipment. However, if you are fit and healthy, love exercise and can take your dog to quiet pathways, this could be the answer to matching your exercise requirements to those of your dog.

For the best results, find people who are doing Canicross (dog-powered cross-country running) and bikejoring (similar with mountain bikes) as a sport to find out what equipment is needed. A harness that allows your dog to run freely without impeding their movement is essential, as is a way of attaching the dog to either you or your bike safely with a quick release mechanism in case of emergency. Harnesses for you to wear while running that do not impede your movement are also important and need to be carefully positioned so you don't injure your back as your dog pulls on the harness.

Some energetic dogs will love the chance to exercise in this way, but running on roads can lead to sore paws and it will cause wear and tear on their joints that could lead to lameness. Ideally, you should run on grass or soft non-stony tracks.

Dogs will need a body similar to wild dogs or wolves to cope with extended periods of running. Dogs that have a more natural shape and a light body with a normal coat will fare better, whereas dogs that have a very heavy coat, a heavy build or a body that causes weight to be borne on small areas of joints (such as dogs whose legs are not straight) are less likely to tolerate long runs and this type of exercise may result in lameness or physical damage. Good training is also needed to ensure your dog is less likely to trip you up or make sudden, accident-causing sideways rushes after other dogs or wildlife.

While a long straight run may be good for physical exercise, remember that it will do nothing to exercise them mentally and so your dog will still need the chance to explore and find interests away from home even after a good run. To combat this, alternate jogging or cycling with days when you go for working walks instead (see page 26).

DOG WALKERS

Finding a good dog walker who will provide safe routine exercise for your dog on a daily basis can be a game-changing option for owners who work all day. They can also be used temporarily if you have an unexpected injury that means you can't go for walks, or at times – having a baby, for example – when all your free time and energy is used up. Even if you usually have plenty of time to walk your dog, finding someone you can trust to walk your dog is a good idea, just in case you can't make it home or one of life's surprises takes you out of your normal routines.

Liking dogs is not enough. The best dog walkers will also have plenty of experience and a deep knowledge of all things canine. They should have a positive and friendly attitude to dogs, rather than being controlling and punitive. They will take only small numbers of dogs on walks at a time so they can give them individual attention and will have decent transport available that allows them to separate each dog during travel. They should be open and honest about what they do and what they know. Be sure to ask plenty of questions, such as what they would do if they lost your dog on a walk, and be happy with their answers before you entrust them with your precious friend.

TREADMILLS

Treadmills are expensive and your dog will need to be trained to use them successfully, but they can provide a way for very active dogs to use up excess energy. However, just like treadmills for humans, they are not much fun and it is inhumane to tie dogs in such a way that they have no choice but to keep walking on one. Dogs can be taught to use a treadmill using treats but it is unlikely that most dogs will want to use them for long. It is really better for all concerned to find a more natural method of exercise for your dog.

CANINE HYDROTHERAPY

Hydrotherapy, where dogs swim in special doggy swimming pools attended by a professional, is useful when weight-bearing exercise is difficult, such as in the case of deformities, rehabilitation from injury, other ailments or aging. Canine hydrotherapy centres are often run by animal physiotherapists who understand which movements and how much exercise will be relevant for your pet. They can be an expensive form of exercise for a normal healthy dog but it may be more beneficial for some dogs, particularly for older dogs who have more difficulties with movement.

It is always best to check the qualifications and experience of the people running the hydrotherapy centre and particularly those who will take your dog for its swim. Most hydrotherapy units allow the owners to be present so be concerned if you are not welcome. Before you go, ask about their methods for getting dogs into the water if they are reluctant so there are no unpleasant surprises when your dog gets there.

Working walks

Physical exercise needs to be balanced by mental activity so that your dog gets the benefit of a more natural way to use up energy and keep fit. Although it is easier for us to walk a dog that does its own thing while we walk along thinking of other things or playing with our phone, this can lead to a disengagement between you and your dog that could eventually result in a poor recall and running off. Your dog may start getting into trouble with other dogs, jumping up at other people walking their dogs, running off after scent trails or chasing livestock instead of interacting with you at points along the walk. Walking your dog when you only engage with them to put the lead on to go home is a wasted opportunity to bond with, train and have fun together. A walk that involves a balance of freedom for your dog and happy interaction with humans will be best for all.

A working walk involves a series of planned activities that happen at random and can help your dog learn to want to be with you at all times instead of running off and getting into trouble elsewhere. It should consist of both interactional activities and some time for freedom and exploration, which gives fun times together combined with some peace to do

their own thing. Plan what you may do during the walk or decide as you go – the more you practice the suggestions for games with toys and training exercises (see pages 29–31), the more activities you will have to share with your dog on walks. The environment may also prompt you to engage in different activities.

Sometimes you or your dog may not feel like a full working walk and you may prefer to be deep in thought and to walk undistracted. This is fine occasionally, and neither of you will mind if activities do not happen sometimes, especially if you are not too routine about when and where you do them.

If you get into the habit of doing various activities at random with your dog, though, sometimes doing more if you have the energy, and sometimes a bit less when you don't, you will both get a lot more out of your walks. As an added bonus, your recall cue will begin to signal that there may be a fun activity on offer and you will find your dog gradually becoming more responsive about coming back. Your dog will also be more tired and fulfilled after the walk and happier in your company and the bond between you will develop.

These working walks are ideal for getting to know a new dog or for educating a young puppy. For adult or elderly dogs, working walks can help keep them fit and interested in life and fun, and even help extend their lives.

A SUGGESTED PLAN FOR A WORKING WALK

Before leaving home, you will need at least two different kinds of high-value, meaty food treats, easily accessible in different pockets, as well as a couple of your dog's favourite toys. You may need to teach your dog how to play with toys on walks (see pages 166–77).

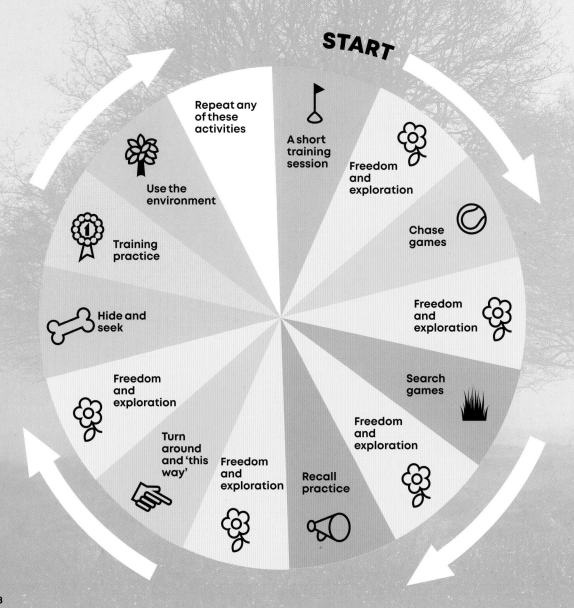

START

A short training session

Freedom and exploration

Chase games

Freedom and exploration

Search games

Freedom and exploration

Recall practice

Freedom and exploration

Turn around and 'this way'

Freedom and exploration

Hide and seek

Training practice

Use the environment

Repeat any of these activities

A SHORT TRAINING SESSION

Start with some lead work practice in a park. You may need to walk to the park on lead anyway, but even if you don't, starting out from the car or house with a quick training session can set the right tone for a working walk and allow you to start off well together, both physically and mentally. Give favourite treats (real meat rather than cereal-based foods) generously for staying with you and make frequent turns to keep things interesting. (If you struggle with loose lead walking, consider employing the services of a good dog trainer to teach you how.) If you are not near a road, reward occasionally with a game with a toy.

If your dog is used to hauling you to the park on the end of the lead and then flying off as soon as you take off the lead, it will take time for them to get used to a different routine. Try not to be disheartened if this doesn't work out so well initially. You may need to work at this for a while, rewarding generously and frequently and keeping things fun and varied to keep their attention before they learn that activities with you can be fun too. It may take a few days or even a week for them to realize there is more fun to be had with you than on their own.

FREEDOM AND EXPLORATION

The mainstay of a dog's walk is freedom to explore and run free. A suitable safe environment and a reliable recall will allow you to let your dog off lead so you can both relax and have some time to yourselves. Dogs really welcome the chance to use their noses to sniff out all the scents left by other creatures in the environment.

A dog's primary sense is that of smell (see page 175) and being set free to find out who or what has passed through that environment recently seems to make them very happy. They may run fast when first released but soon settle down to a steadier pace that allows them to stop and sniff anything interesting that they encounter along the way, usually the scents left behind by other animals and birds. We can never know what it feels like to be able to smell in as much detail as dogs can but they certainly seem to relish every moment of their scented explorations. It may be their equivalent of reading the newspaper or watching video footage of the action that happened before they got there.

CHASE GAMES

Next you might play some chase games, rewarding your dog for bringing the toy back to you with either another game or a tasty treat (see page 80). Play vigorously for a short time and then resume your walk.

SEARCH GAMES

After another freedom and exploration session, a few search games will hold their interest and get them focused on working with you again. Hold your dog's collar and throw a toy into long grass. Help your dog to seek it out and reward well when the toy is found. Increase the complexity and distance involved gradually as your dog's experience develops. For example, you might throw a toy into leaves or other cover while your dog is looking elsewhere (pay close attention to exactly where it lands so you know where it is in case you are the one who has to retrieve it) or drop a toy as you walk through open ground, sending your dog back to find it on the path you have trodden. As long as you increase the complexity and distance gradually, your dog should really enjoy this game. Eventually, try with different toys and objects. Something really useful to teach is to 'find' lost keys, but practice with a spare set first. Due to the anatomy of your dog's eyes, they can only see in the colour range of blues and yellow and cannot easily distinguish between red and green. This makes a search for a red toy on green grass more difficult, so start with an easily seen toy and move on to red toys on grass for an experienced dog that has got used to searching with their nose only.

RECALL PRACTICE

After giving your dog some more free time, you could do some recall practice, calling your dog several times and rewarding well with a tasty treat or a game with a toy, and then allowing them freedom to run off again.

TURN AROUND AND 'THIS WAY'

It will be more fun for your dog if you keep them guessing as to which way you are going, rather than following a familiar route every day. Give your dog a signal that you are about to change direction or go down a different trail. If you do this often, sometimes turning around and going back the other way, or sometimes taking a different path to the one your dog is on, you will find that your dog becomes very responsive to that signal. This could be useful in an emergency when your dog is heading for something that is intriguing to them, but you would rather they move away from. You may find it works better than your recall signal.

HIDE AND SEEK

Hide and seek games, played with people, tap into your dog's natural desire to keep family together and to know where other members of their group have gone. If you are walking with someone, hold your dog and ask them to hide. Make sure it is somewhere easy at first such as behind a nearby tree. Send your dog to 'find' the missing person and celebrate with them when the person is 'found'. Gradually increase the complexity until your dog can track and find someone even if they did not see where they went. Your dog will learn to use their incredible sense of smell to track them down. Dogs usually love playing hide and seek with family members, and it will help strengthen the bond between you all and leave your dog well exercised and contented. If you are walking alone, make a treasure square by hiding tasty treats or a favourite toy in an area of long grass and help your dog to find them.

TRAINING PRACTICE

Break off occasionally for a short session of training practice. These sessions can incorporate anything your dog has previously learned, or you could teach your dog something new providing your surroundings are quiet and not distracting. Have fun with your dog, running through their repertoire of training cues and tricks and reward well with a tasty treat, activity or game with a toy. Keep these sessions light-hearted and positive and you will have a dog that learns to love these fun breaks on walks. For more information on how to train positively, see page 196.

For more information on how to train positively, see page 196.

USE THE ENVIRONMENT

After you have been doing working walks for a while, you could look around you for props to use. A fallen tree could be the perfect climbing frame, or a patch of scrubland might be the ideal place to run a search for a toy (taking care to avoid sharp or dangerous objects, of course). A wood may make a good place for the family to hide out for your dog to find, or a shallow stream could be a good place to throw floating toys for your dog to fetch. Making use of natural places in this way keeps things interesting for you both.

Use the activities suggested here at times when it may be difficult to keep your dog's attention or there may be consequences if your dog does not stay close. For example, practice with your dog walking closely beside you on lead if people are approaching who have small children or who may be worried about a running dog. If your dog is focused on doing fun activities with you, they will be less likely to get into trouble.

Electronic monitoring

There are plenty of different trackers available that will allow you to monitor your dog's activity levels and other measures of wellness. They attach to the collar and will provide information such as distance travelled and time spent active and playing, walking, running and sleeping. A waterproof tracker is useful if your dog loves water.

Most attentive dog owners have a sixth sense for detecting when their pet is not well, but these activity trackers can give you an early warning that all may not be well if your dog starts to slow down, sleep more, and become less active, as well as giving you data to

take to your vet. In addition to having a practical use, it is interesting to see how far your dog travels each day and also how active it is compared to you. You will need to remember to recharge the battery after a few months, although some batteries last as long as a year.

Some trackers have GPS which allows you to find your dog if it is lost, but these trackers usually have more rudimentary monitoring functions and are more expensive to buy. An additional monthly subscription is needed to keep the GPS activated, so research the monthly cost of this before you purchase. GPS trackers also have a much shorter battery life, measured in terms of days rather than months. If you take your dog's collar off when you are at home, it should not be too much trouble to plug it in to recharge, but it can be a nuisance to remove the tracker every few days and it is easy to forget. GPS trackers can also be quite large and heavy, so for small dogs it may be better to attach one to a harness instead of a collar. For all their inconvenience, though, having the reassurance of a GPS signal to help you know where to start your search during those initial moments of dread and panic when you realize your dog is missing has to be worth the extra cost and effort.

Although trackers with GPS can give you great peace of mind if you allow your dog off lead, they should not be used as a substitute for training a good recall and for keeping your dog actively engaged with you on a walk (see page 26).

Exercise and the short-faced dog

Dogs with short faces have been purposely bred, whether consciously or not, to have a flat face and big eyes that resemble a human face or baby. Pugs, English Bulldogs, Cavalier King Charles Spaniels and French Bulldogs are examples. Sadly, all pay a price for this human choice with a breathing apparatus that is compromised, sometimes to the point of needing surgical intervention. Snoring is common in these breeds as soft tissue blocks their airways when they relax into sleep, which is why they will often sleep with their heads propped up against a wall or on a pillow in an effort to get sufficient air in to stay asleep rather than wake up through suffocation. Even during the day, short-faced dogs often struggle to get enough

oxygen into their lungs to feel comfortable, especially in hot weather, and, consequently, they are often not able to exercise as much as other dogs, especially as they get older.

Care must be taken when exercising short-faced dogs not to overexert them or get them so excited that they collapse or faint. A short, slow walk may be all some of them can manage and it is important not to overtire them or continue to ask them to exercise past the point that is comfortable for them.

Take extra care in hot weather when oxygen concentrations may be lower and give your dog plenty of opportunity to rest in the shade during hot, sunny days.

Harmful exercise

It is possible to give your dog too much exercise if it is the wrong sort or if it is encouraged way past the point when your dog would naturally stop. Dogs that want to play all the time and have a strong working ability or play drive that causes them to play intensely for long periods can be easily persuaded into prolonged active or stimulating games that could be harmful if played to excess. Chase games (see page 170), for example, which provide high arousal and mindless exercise, can be harmful if played to the exclusion of all other exercise, so always balance these with plenty of other types of play and training to engage your dog's brain and help it to feel calm.

Always be careful when playing games in a confined space where a chasing dog may not see the edge of a low table or door as it speeds towards the toy. Similarly, avoid throwing or playing with toys in such a way that your dog may twist, fall or hurt itself while playing, particularly if you have an enthusiastic dog that will try to reach any toy thrown. Similarly, avoid allowing your dog to exercise in places where falls or injuries are possible, for example, near to cliff edges or where there may be broken glass or sharp objects.

Consider, too, whether your dog has a body shape that compromises its physical movement. For example, Dachshunds and other dogs with long bodies and

short legs can hurt themselves when jumping off sofas or when going up and down stairs as puppies. Taking special care of dogs with a compromised ability to move and exercise will prevent pain for your dog and expensive visits to the vet.

Finally, take a look at the physical activities your dog does on a regular basis, such as jumping in and out of cars. Think about the wear and tear on particular parts of your dog's body at those times and consider whether too much of that activity will result in a repetitive strain or arthritis in later life. If the answer could be yes, think of ways to vary or change those activities to cause less harm to your dog.

Exercise through the ages

Young puppies up to the age of puberty (this usually occurs at around six months, although can be much later for larger dogs) have soft bones and cartilage that can be damaged and deformed by too much prolonged walking on a lead. Puppies are better left to run free in a safe place where they can play and exercise themselves. Most puppies will stop and lie down for a rest when their bodies are tired. However, some pups, especially those from working lines or that are easily excited into games, get so involved with the game that they continue to play long after they should have stopped. This can result in physical exhaustion and injury. Gentle short play sessions lasting less than three minutes are good, as are slow short exploratory

walks to get used to the world (be prepared to carry them when they get tired), but long walks or runs should be avoided until their bodies are ready to cope with the mechanical stresses involved.

During adolescence, a dog's body is maturing and is capable of a lot more physical exertion. Just as their need for exercise increases, setting them free becomes more difficult as they now have the mind of an adolescent that is focused on the outside world. This is likely to continue until they mature at about 18 months to 2 years of age. Finding safe places where they can burn off their teenage enthusiasm and desire to explore will help to make them more content at home, as well as happier and nicer to live with.

Old age brings its own challenges and, with it, the desire to exercise gradually diminishes. This is a time for short walks to different places to keep their interest peaked and to help them get the exercise they need to keep them moving. You will need to be prepared to walk slowly again and go out for frequent short walks, as with a puppy, but encouraging old dogs to exercise and keep interested in life will help keep them well. Since their sense of smell is the last to go, taking old dogs on walks to places where other animals have been will give them lovely experiences when most other things in their lives have lost their appeal. Old dogs are inclined to wander off and get lost though, moving surprisingly fast in the wrong direction if you happen to get distracted for a while, so be prepared to keep an eye on them at all times. Fitting a GPS tracker (see page 32) to their collar may be a good idea.

CHAPTER 2

Combating disease

The small Jack Russell Terrier leapt in the air, jumping and spinning and snapping her teeth together in a frenzy, as if trying to catch a swarm of tiny unseen insects.

She would rest for a minute or two and then start again, over and over as if desperate to bring those unseen flying creatures to order. Careful questioning of her distraught owners revealed that this 'craziness' had been going on for less than a week. Before this behaviour started, she was a normal happy two-year-old, living a life of games and walks and padding about their house and garden with her brother who she was raised with.

Sudden onset behaviour problems in an otherwise normal healthy dog usually have their origins in some kind of physiological or health-related problem and so it was important to find out what had happened just before the problem had started. 'Nothing', answered the owners. 'It was a normal Sunday. We got up late, had a late lunch, we went out to friends in the afternoon and the "craziness" was happening when we got back.' More detailed questioning of their memories of Sunday morning revealed that one of the owners had given both dogs their monthly dose of a spot-on medication designed to protect them against fleas and ticks. This treatment is placed between the shoulder blades so that the dog cannot lick it. Even closer questioning revealed something she had forgotten – she left the two dogs alone after treatment

and had returned to the room to find the female dog licking the medication site on the neck of her brother. The owner had shouted at her to stop, but she may have already ingested a good amount of a drug meant only for external application.

Fortunately, there was no long-term damage and the 'craziness' stopped a few days later, about the time taken for the drug to be excreted by her young liver. Her owners were not clueless or unintelligent, but they had grown complacent about the use of a routine medication used many times before and known to be safe. In reality, drugs used for any medical care or prevention should be used under a set of specific constraints and any departure from this can lead to harm. These powerful chemicals need to be used with care and dedication to the instructions.

Preventing disease or acting fast to tackle it when it arrives is essential for your dog's wellbeing. Adequate control of common contagious viruses, bacteria and parasites and ensuring chemical and other challenges to the body are kept to a minimum takes knowledge and careful balancing. Following the methods in this book will, of course, help your dog to develop a strong immune system, but all dogs will need a little extra help at times.

Naturally healthy

You cannot do anything about your dog's genetic propensity for certain diseases (except at the purchasing stage) or prevent accidental injury, but it should otherwise be possible to keep your dog healthy most of the time.

The best protection against any disease is good health that helps enhance your dog's natural defenses.

- **Feeding a good diet will boost your dog's immunity and give all the essential building blocks for a healthy body.**
- **Providing sufficient opportunities for exercise will help keep your dog fit.**

- **Allowing enough time for sleep and rest while balancing with fun, play and mind games, plus keeping stress at bay with sensitive handling and an emotionally supportive environment, will avoid weakening your dog's immune system and help them fight disease.**

There are no guarantees and you are unlikely to avoid all illnesses throughout your dog's lifetime, but we should not underestimate the power of most animal's bodies to keep themselves healthy given the right conditions. Doing our best to provide those conditions is the best way to stay out of the veterinary clinic.

Vaccinations

Vaccines attempt to protect your dog from potentially fatal contagious diseases that may be prevalent in your area. To make a vaccine, the pathogen (usually a virus or bacteria) is killed or severely weakened before being injected under the skin. Sometimes just the toxins the pathogen produces are used or even some of its surface proteins. The vaccine causes a challenge to your puppy's or dog's immune system which reacts by producing antibodies. The response is similar to that needed in the real disease and trains the immune system so that it is ready to respond appropriately.

A puppy gets some antibodies from its mother and her milk, but these are quickly replaced when its own immune system starts up and learns to respond to pathogens the puppy encounters throughout its own life. It is usual to give a series (usually two, sometimes three) of vaccination injections to a young puppy between six and twelve weeks of age to provide immunity against the core life-threatening diseases, namely canine distemper (CD), infectious hepatitis, canine adenovirus (CAV) and parvovirus type 2 (CPV-2). Puppies may also be routinely vaccinated against leptospirosis, kennel cough and rabies. Since

there is a possibility that these early vaccinations do not take due to lingering maternal antibodies, it may be best to give a booster vaccination at six or twelve months of age, around the time of the routine first health check (see WSAVA guidelines below) or, even better, to do a titre test (see below) at four to six months to see if the initial vaccinations have taken and, if not, to give a booster.

Early vaccination of puppies not only protects the individual but, if enough dogs are vaccinated in a community, it reduces the overall prevalence of the disease and makes contact with infectious dogs less likely. This is important since although vaccination is effective in the vast majority of dogs (approximately 98 per cent)[1], there is a small percentage who do not become immune after vaccination (immunity is only conferred if the dog's immune system responds to it).

Another reason for vaccination is that some boarding establishments require an up-to-date vaccination record before they will take your dog, as will some forms of travel, especially travel overseas (although some will accept 'evidence' in the form of titre test results too).

A BONE OF CONTENTION

Few would dispute that a programme of vaccination early in life is necessary to protect the health of puppies. However, there is some controversy around whether or not to give repeated annual booster vaccinations throughout life. Since vaccination is not totally without risk, veterinarians are often caught between the desire to make sure dogs are fully protected against life-threatening diseases and not wanting to give unnecessary challenges to a sensitive immune system. Side effects range from adverse reactions at the injection site to the more serious (but rare) cases of short-lived lethargy, swelling, itching, shortness of breath, vomiting, diarrhoea or collapse. In some dogs, immune-mediated haemolytic anaemia may occur and since vaccines affect the immune system and microbiome[2] any disease process could be affected, although this is very difficult to prove.

All dog owners need to be aware of the World Small Animal Veterinary Association guidelines for vaccinations for the most severe and life-threatening diseases[3]. The guidelines are put together and kept up to date by an international independent team of eminent veterinarians. They state that, after the 6–12 month booster injection, further vaccines should not be given any more frequently than every three years, since the duration of immunity is many years and may be up to the lifetime of the pet. To help you make a fully informed decision, please refer to these guidelines in consultation with your dog's veterinarian.

BLOOD TITRES

The immune system is complex and scientists are still learning about its intricacies. After vaccination, it is difficult to know if your dog's immune system has responded and is able to make its own antibodies if challenged by the disease. One way to determine this is through tests called titres that determine the level of antibody present in a small blood sample.

Titre tests are easy to do and can be done for the core contagious diseases (CDV, CPV-2 and CAV), although they do require a blood sample, take up veterinary staff time and can be more expensive than a routine vaccine. If antibodies are present, there is no need for a booster. An annual titre test can remove the need for routine booster vaccinations and so prevent unnecessary challenges to your dog's immune system and other bodily processes. The problem with titre tests is that a low count does not necessarily mean the immune system has forgotten how to respond, just that high levels of antibodies to these diseases were not being produced when the blood test was taken. This would then give a false negative result.

In addition, we do not know if antibodies in the blood are always indicative of complete protection for all diseases, so although titre results strongly suggest immunity, they cannot guarantee it completely. Overall, however, until this field of science develops further, titre tests may be our best hope for keeping our dogs healthy and reducing repeated challenges to the immune system via vaccination that may not be needed.

LEPTOSPIROSIS

Leptospirosis is a serious disease caused by the *Leptospira* bacteria found in nearly all soil and water worldwide. It is more common in warmer climates and places with high rainfall, standing water and mud, but it can occur anywhere. Whether you decide to vaccinate your dog against it is a decision to be made in conjunction with your veterinarian who will know about local disease conditions.

The efficacy of the vaccine can be variable, being either short lasting or limited, and there have been some reports of adverse reactions to the vaccine (the WSAVA suggests not to vaccinate toy dogs against leptospirosis because of their high levels of adverse reactions to the vaccine). At present, there is no meaningful test for Leptospirosis immunity and a vaccination for this disease may be needed every year depending on local disease conditions.

NOSODES

Nosodes are the homeopathic equivalent of conventional vaccines. They are prepared by taking a tiny quantity of the disease then diluting and shaking it until there is no detectable traces of the original substance left. Proponents for homeopathy maintain that nosodes represent a safe, effective alternative to conventional vaccine.

Nosodes may be safer but are they effective or will they leave your dog unprotected? Unfortunately, evidence that homeopathy is effective is not detectable by scientific methods[4] and the whole practice of homeopathic treatment is controversial.

Homeopathy has been largely discredited in the UK since NHS England recommended that practitioners should stop prescribing because of a lack of robust evidence of clinical effectiveness[5] and it may well be one of those branches of medicine that were thought to be effective but were later proven otherwise.

Parasites

Common parasites such as worms, ticks and fleas need to be controlled with adequate medication. However, there may be no need for repeated and regular treatment for a dog 'as a precaution' since this may mean you will be giving chemicals unnecessarily. A more considered approach could be beneficial.

Worms are common in pregnant females and young puppies, and both are in need of adequate worm management. Once a dog is a healthy adult, a faecal egg count (via a faeces sample) can be done for round worm and lung worm to see if medication is really needed. Lung worm can be potentially fatal, so regular testing is important. Both types of worm can be quickly cleared from your dog's system with an anthelmintic – a medicine that kills or expels parasitic worms (helminths) – available from your veterinary practice.

For a more natural approach than using routine pharmaceutical anthelmintics, herbal preparations and Diatomaceous Earth (a sand made up of the shells of millions of fossilized diatoms) may be useful and may help in the control of tapeworms if needed, too. Only use food-grade Diatomaceous Earth, which has all the smallest dust removed to avoid problems if it is inhaled, and always seek advice from a veterinary professional experienced in more holistic methods.

FLEAS

There are plenty of easy chemical treatments for fleas, but do not underestimate the chemical load they put on your dog's body or the devastating effect they may have on invertebrates in the environment (such as bees), not to mention that we do not necessarily have all the answers yet and some chemicals that had been licensed as safe for use have now been withdrawn.

A statement has recently been issued by the US Food and Drug Administration warning owners and veterinarians about products containing isoxazoline having the potential for neurologic adverse events in dogs. This includes at least six products previously given licenses and thought to be safe. The accepted norm is to give regular treatment, often as a spot-on medication at the back of the neck, but prevention is better than cure and a healthy dog may not need routine treatment.

More holistic methods involve keeping a careful watch for signs of fleas (black specks at the base of the neck and tail which turn red on a damp tissue, or finding a small but itchy flea bite on yourself) and taking immediate action. Essential oil mixes put through the coat can be effective, but take care with this and get expert advice before doing so. Diatomaceous Earth in the coat can desiccate any existing fleas and eggs and this can also be used in the home (on carpet, bedding and between floorboards and so on to kill fleas and their eggs), or bicarbonate of soda can be used instead.

Flea traps can also be useful. Once you see signs of fleas, it is important to treat your home as well as your dog. If you can actually see fleas on your dog, there will be many more in the environment (where they wait until they have digested their recent blood meal and lay eggs before hopping back on), and at that stage, aggressive treatment with pharmaceuticals will be needed. In addition, remember to look out for other pets sharing the same space, in particular cats. Cat fleas (*Ctenocephalides felis*) are a different species to dog fleas (*Ctenocephalides canis*) but are not very host-specific so can often be found living on dogs.

TICKS

Ticks can crawl onto your dog from vegetation frequented by livestock and wild animals and are more prevalent in the warmer months. Ticks latch on, bore a tiny hole in your dog's skin (or yours!) and suck their blood until they are full, when they drop off and prepare to lay eggs. Some may be carrying a tick-borne virus (the percentage that are doing so will depend on the local disease conditions).

If you find a tick on your dog (or yourself) do not squeeze it while it is latched on. Blood already in the tick's gut that may contain disease can get pushed back into the dog's (or your) blood stream.

It is essential to remove ticks carefully with a special tool called a tick hook (available from vets, pet shops or online). This twists the mouthparts out of the skin without the need to touch the body, thus preventing any infection. This method also helps to prevent the tick's mouthparts breaking off and staying in the skin which could cause an abscess.

Dogs can wear special collars, which deliver low levels of pesticides, in heavily infested areas where tick-borne viruses are suspected, but these are a disaster for any invertebrates living in the same environment. Essential oil sprays may be better but take advice from an holistic vet before using.

Protection and profit

Be aware that the main purpose of the companies producing vaccines and drugs for parasite control is profit, and while they will be working within scientific boundaries, they may be giving protocols that may be in excess of what is needed for your particular dog. These are very useful products when necessary. However, it is essential to be well informed about how often booster vaccinations and repeat wormers or other medication are needed, and to get this information from sources other than the companies selling the products is essential. This allows you to make an informed choice and keep the amount of artificial chemicals going into or onto your dog to a minimum.

Veterinary treatment

There will be times when your dog is unwell or has an accident. At these times, we need to take quick advantage of and be very grateful for the excellent care given by veterinary surgeons and supporting staff. We are lucky to live in times when so much can be done medically to save our pets and to have veterinary professionals who are so well educated and proficient. It is better to seek a veterinary opinion as soon as you notice something is wrong. If you are in tune with your dog, this can be very early on in a disease or ailment and it is always better to catch and treat potential problems early.

Health insurance

With an increase in the extent of treatments available has come an increased cost. Health insurance for your dog may be a good idea if you do not have the savings to pay for extensive treatment should it becomes necessary. Be sure to check the policy and what will and will not be covered before you buy and be aware that it will get more expensive to cover an ageing dog due to the increased risk of them getting ailments. At the very least, all dog owners should have third party liability insurance, just in case their dog causes an accident for which they are held financially responsible. Some dog charities and organizations offer this as part of their membership but it is wise to check payout limits and other details carefully.

CHAPTER 3

Good nutrition

As soon as their front door opened, the young black Cocker Spaniel threw himself enthusiastically at me, tail wagging furiously.

I noticed his grey coat, which on closer inspection was due to copious white dandruff, and as I entered an overwhelming smell of dog in this otherwise pristine house made me wrinkle my nostrils. His gentle owner had called me about a possessive aggression problem that was scaring her and bringing him into conflict at most crossover points with his humans. This dog was indulged and had plenty of everything but had a brain and attitude ready to work all day every day. Life on his silken cushion had become boring so he livened it up with competition games he coerced his owners into playing over toys, chews and any item unlucky enough to find itself on the floor.

In answer to a routine question about diet, I discovered this adult dog was fed only on cooked skinned chicken breast. 'He won't eat anything else and he would starve rather than eat dog food', the owner said. Looking at his portly appearance I could see that this bright dog had cleverly trained his indulgent owner to feed him only what he most enjoyed and plenty of it. Luckily for her bank balance he hadn't yet been introduced to fillet steak.

So, is it bad to feed dogs on meat alone? How much vegetable matter is enough? Do dogs need grains and other carbohydrates? What did dogs evolve to eat and what is 'natural'? These and many more questions have been at the forefront of dog owners' minds since we started thinking harder about our own diet, reading labels on dog food packets, and wondering what really is the best food for our pets.

Good nutrition and the correct quantities of food are two of the cornerstones of optimal health and getting it right for your dog is one of the most important things you can do to improve their wellbeing. Making the right choices in this area can make the world of difference to your dog's health and longevity, but a clear path of how to proceed is not always obvious. The information given here will provide a solid base on which to make careful choices about what goes into your dog's body and hence what building blocks they will have to grow, stay healthy and provide energy for a fulfilled life.

What would dogs eat 'naturally'?

Dogs do not 'naturally' exist in the wild as, say, wolves and lions do, so there is much debate over what is natural for them. Dogs that have become feral tend to hunt small rodents and scavenge to survive, eating whatever nutritious material they can get hold of, usually from the waste that humans have discarded. The dog's closest cousin, the grey wolf (*Canis lupus*), is a true carnivore that predates on other animals, such as deer and rodents, but it is not the ancestor of the dog – both dogs and wolves evolved from a common ancestor millions of years ago.

When animals were first being classified, scientists examined their bodies and behaviour to see what they ate and, hence, which group they should be placed in. Dogs have an anatomy for eating and digestion that most resembles members of the order Carnivora (in Latin 'flesh devourers') that live by hunting and eating the flesh of other animals. They have the pointed and jagged teeth necessary for tearing and slicing meat rather than the flat grinding surfaces found in animals that eat mostly plants. Their jaws move up and down to grab and gulp large pieces of meat, rather than moving from side to side to crush plants and other fibrous material.

In addition, dogs have a much shorter digestive tract than herbivores, with a reduced ability to ferment plant matter to extract all the nutrients. The length of an animal's gut reflects the length of time for digestion, and hence what they evolved to eat, and a dog's digestive tract is not as long that of a true omnivore (an animal that evolved to eat both plants and meat), a group that includes pigs and humans.

Dogs have also retained some of the instinctive propensities for behaviour that might allow them to catch and kill their own dinner if thrown into the wild, although many breeds have bodies that make them too slow or the wrong shape to be effective.

In truth, man has been selectively breeding dogs for their working ability for generations without much thought about feeding or digestion. Dogs have been fed on a huge variety of different diets, often consisting of the foods that humans did not want themselves. This natural experiment has shown that dogs can exist on many different diets and can utilize just about any food we want to feed them. However, this does not mean all diets are equivalent in nutritional value or that all diets will provide your dog with optimum health.

At present, the jury is out on what is the best diet for our canine companions and the science is inconclusive on proof either way. However, your decision on what to feed your dog could have a huge impact on both the length of their life and their state of health. Dogs' bodies and behaviours seem to show a natural carnivorous bias, so if you want to give your dog a long healthy life and feed 'naturally', deciding whether to feed them predominantly on meat, as you would a carnivore, or whether to include other less expensive products such as cereals, is an important consideration for any owner.

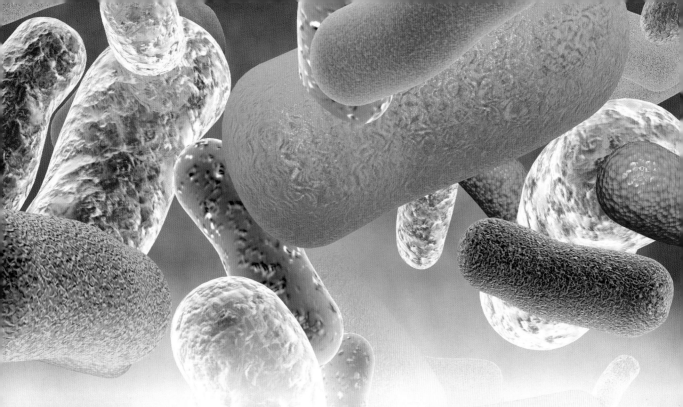

The microbiota and its importance

The microbiota of the gut is the ecosystem of organisms – consisting of bacteria, fungi, yeasts and other microorganisms – that live in the digestive tract and play an essential role in keeping an animal healthy and happy (the microbiome is the genetic material the microbiota contains). Although there is very little data on canine microbiota, faeces samples show that the microflora (species and predominance) of the canine gut is similar to that of the human gut[1].

Although we do not yet understand the exact role of the gut microbiota, we do know it plays a major role in health and disease. Gut microbes influence the immune system, protect against opportunistic pathogens, have a role in harvesting nutrients and energy from food, and ferment non-digestible carbohydrates. Disruption of the gut microbiota is associated with obesity, diabetes, inflammatory bowel diseases, and autoimmune diseases[2].

It is known that the microbiota is more effective if it is diverse (contains many different species) and there is usually an association between reduced diversity and disease. This may be because different species of organism have different functions and if environmental influences, antibiotics or dietary changes cause a reduction in diversity, other microbes with a similar function can compensate for the function of the missing species. Consequently, diversity seems to be a generally good indicator of a healthy gut and hence a healthy dog[3].

Of all the environmental factors studied to date, long-term diet has the biggest effect on the quality and diversity of the human gut microbiota[4]. If we extrapolate this to dogs, choosing the right diet for your dog is of upmost importance. In a small study undertaken to determine the effects of a raw meat-based diet compared with a commercial kibble-

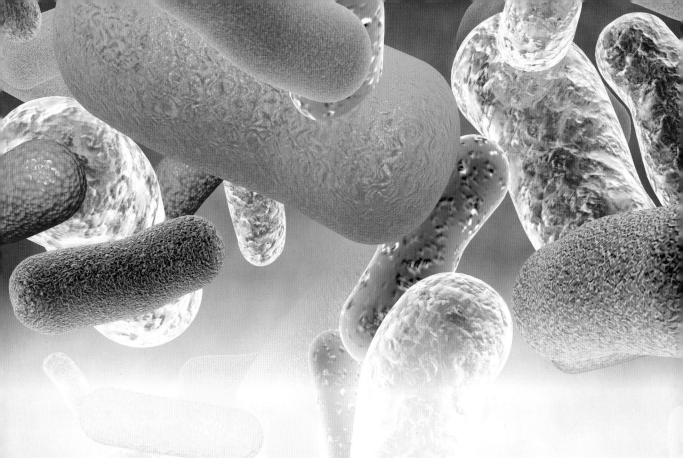

based diet, it was found that the raw meat-based diet promoted a more balanced growth of bacterial communities and more diversity in the microbiota in comparison to a kibble-based diet[5].

PRE AND PROBIOTICS – ARE THEY NECESSARY?

A prebiotic is a non-digestible food that helps useful microorganisms already resident to flourish in the colon (this definition can also be used for non-digestible dietary fibre). A prebiotic can, however, only encourage growth of species already present in the gut.

Probiotics are live microbial supplements that have a beneficial effect by improving intestinal microbial balance. Probiotics are not normally necessary unless your dog is fed largely on processed or sterile foods. If mostly fresh food is consumed, the gut microbiota will have a natural source of microbes without the need

to supplement[6]. If, however, the normal microbiota is disturbed, for example if your dog is given a course of antibiotics, probiotics may be needed.

When choosing a probiotic, look for those with many strains of favourable bacteria (eg *Lactobacillus, Bifidobacterium, Saccharomyces, Enterococcus, Streptococcus, Pediococcus, Leuconostoc, Bacillus, Escherichia coli*) to ensure a wide diversity of species[7].

BEWARE

Probiotics may be harmful in dogs that have a weakened immune system or a leaky gut so do seek professional veterinary advice before using these supplements.

What's really inside your dog's food?

Always read the label. Your dog's health and wellbeing depend on you taking the time to read and thoroughly understand what is going into the food your dog is eating rather than taking for granted that dog food manufacturers want the very best for your dog like you do. Of course, some manufacturers are very reputable and ethically minded, but it is a sad fact of life that when money and animals merge, profits can be considered above welfare.

Unfortunately, dog food labelling is not always easy to understand so it is important to be well-informed and know what you are reading when looking at labels. Although the food may look and smell good, and your dog may find it appetizing, it is important to ask yourself what is really inside the food that your beloved pet is eating every day and just how nourishing it is. If you can't see and smell the individual ingredients, you cannot really know about the type and quality of the ingredients or how fresh they are. This is particularly important if the ingredients are highly processed and you cannot tell what the product is made from.

LABELLING REGULATIONS

Laws govern what manufacturers must print on food labelling and this is different in different countries. For example, there are federal regulations in the US, enforced by the US Food and Drug Administration, although some states enforce their own regulations, and many have adopted the more specific regulations established by the Association of American Feed Control Officials (AAFCO). In the UK and Europe, manufacturers are subject to European Union regulations and these regulations are enforced by various legislative bodies, such as the Food Standards Agency in the UK. Trade bodies, such as the Pet Food Manufacturers Association (PFMA) in the UK, work in conjunction with FEDIAF, the European pet food industry's governing body. All of these organizations publish details of their regulations.

Much like human food labels, ingredients must be listed in descending order by weight, so the product's main ingredient will be listed first, followed by the second and so forth. Beware, though. A practice known as 'splitting' can get around this regulation. For example, if you were selling a food made predominantly of cereal but wanted the first ingredient to be meat to encourage buyers, you could legally put two types of cereal into the food with the combined weight of both outweighing the meat portion. Because the different cereals can be listed separately and individually weigh less than the meat, they can be listed further down the ingredients list. Meat can be listed as the first ingredient, giving the impression that it's the predominant ingredient.

THE SALT DIVIDE

One way to tell how much, or how little, of an ingredient is in a dog food is to use the salt content as a guide. Salt is toxic at high levels and so it will never be added to dog food at levels of more than one per cent. Since you know this, look for it in the ingredients list and see which ingredients are listed AFTER salt. This will tell you that they are added to the food at a level of less than one per cent. Sometimes glossy photos on the front of a dog food packet indicate, for example, that the food contains cranberries or wild venison. If they appear after salt in the ingredients list you can discount them – although they have been added to the food, they are present in very low quantities.

BEWARE PRODUCT DESCRIPTIONS

Labels can be hard to understand. The diagram opposite shows what the packet contains when labelled according to UK, EU and US regulations (I have used chicken as an example, but it could be any ingredient).

ARTISTIC LICENSE

Whether a company is selling pet food or laundry detergent, it is the job of marketeers to excite interest in a product and to encourage customers to buy it. Consequently, information on dog food labels, apart from the information that is required by law, is often selective and will only tell you what the manufacturer wants you to know.

You may be surprised to know, for example, that there is no regulation of the content of foods labelled as 'premium', 'ultra-premium', 'gourmet', 'hypoallergenic' or even 'natural'. These words are more about marketing than about a technical description. There is no regulation for such products to contain any different or higher-quality ingredients, nor are they held up to a higher nutritional standard than any other complete and balanced products. This is why it pays to read the list of ingredients and to really think about the nutritional quality contained within the food you are feeding your dog.

'FLAVOURED WITH CHICKEN'
= no chicken needs to be in this product as long as it has sufficient flavour* to be detected

'CHICKEN DINNER'
= the product only has to contain 25% (US) or 26% (EU) chicken**

'WITH CHICKEN'
= the product only has to contain 4% (US) or 3% (EU) chicken

BRAND

3kg

'RICH IN CHICKEN'
= the product only has to contain 14% chicken (US & EU)

* flavour used in dog food is often a 'digest' – protein that has been broken down or hydrolyzed with heat, enzymes and/or acids to form a concentrated flavour that is very appetizing to dogs.
** other terms could be used instead of 'dinner' such as 'platter', 'entrée', 'nuggets' and 'formula'.

IS 'MEAT' MEAT?

Bear in mind that all meats listed on dog food labels are not equal. You may be reassured to see meat as the main ingredient, but ask yourself what type of meat it is and where it has come from. If you imagine succulent pieces of beef or chicken that you might eat yourself and that are even shown on the packaging, take a closer look.

The label may list 'freshly prepared meat' as the main ingredient – this is an industry term for meat that has been mechanically separated from a carcass by being put through a deboning machine, ground to reduce particle size, heated to destroy pathogens, centrifuged to remove water and fat and concentrated by vacuum evaporation. The meat slurry that is left is called 'freshly prepared meat'. It is a highly nutritious product, although some of the nutrition will have been lost in the processing, but it is unlikely to be what you were imagining when you first read the term.

Another ingredient that may be listed on the dog food labels is 'meat and animal derivatives'.

This is defined as all the fleshy parts of slaughtered warm-blooded land animals, fresh or preserved by appropriate treatment, and all products and derivatives of the processing of the carcass or parts of the carcass of warm-blooded land animals. This can also be a very nutritious product if the meat being used is high quality and comes from a good source, but, just like 'freshly prepared meat', you have no real idea of the quality of meat or even its origins.

When a dog food product is processed to the point where no ingredient is identifiable, it is not possible to tell the quality of the ingredients without sending it away to be analysed. Buying a processed food means you have to put your faith in the manufacturer and hope that there has been no cost-cutting or any other reason, accidental or deliberate, for unacceptable ingredients to have ended up in the product. Researching the brand and manufacturer can help you determine which are reputable and less likely to cut corners in making their products but you can never be absolutely certain about what your dog is eating.

Processed diets and canned food

Historically, pet dogs were often fed on food left over from human meals. The nutritional quality of these meals would have reflected the quality of the food their owners were eating and could afford, but today's leftover foods may contain sugars, additives, carbohydrates and processed foods which are bad for your dog's health.

Canned dog food first appeared in 1922 and the first kibble-type foods became available in the 1950s. Commercially prepared dog food flourished and by the 1960s it was big business. As well as the homogenous nature of canned food and kibble, both the canning and kibble-making process use high temperatures to sterilize and help to preserve the food from decay. There is some concern that the Maillard Reaction (the reaction between proteins and sugars at high temperatures) – which is responsible for the browning of meat and the darkened crusts on loaves of bread – produces acrylamide which is a carcinogen (a cancer-causing substance). In addition, high temperatures and the additional high pressures necessary for the extrusion process needed to make kibble have some undesirable effects which include reducing the quality of the proteins and fats, decreasing palatability and losing some vitamins[8].

Flavouring and colouring then need to be added to make these foods palatable and kibble is often coated with fats and flavour to encourage dogs to eat it. Synthetic vitamins need to be added back in to replace those that have been lost. Nothing can be done about the reduction of protein and fat quality however and one wonders what other detrimental effects this very unnatural process has on the quality of the kibble being created.

Due to the reduced quality of the nutrients in processed foods and all the additives and preservatives that are necessary to make it palatable, some have likened feeding dogs kibble and processed food to humans eating nothing but take-away meals. While it is perfectly possible to do this for a short time, the long-term consequences of eating these foods are well documented for humans but not yet for dogs. If you want to know more about the effects of eating junk food on humans, watch the *Super Size Me* documentary by Morgan Spurlock, which is available to view on YouTube.

Preservatives

Preservatives are ingredients added to a food to slow down the natural process of decay. These can be antimicrobials (which block the growth of bacteria, moulds and yeasts) and antioxidants (which slow the oxidation of fats and oils that makes food rancid). Unfortunately, a legal loophole exists where dog food manufacturers only have to disclose the ingredients that they themselves add, so any chemicals previously added to component products may not be listed. This is a grey area and another reason why you may never know exactly what is in processed dog food.

ARTIFICIAL PRESERVATIVES

BHA (butylated hydroxyanisole or E320) and BHT (butylated hydroxytoluene or E321) are among the most common artificial antioxidants used in pet foods. Studies have shown that these chemicals can be carcinogenic in quantity and responsible for changes in behaviour[9, 10, 11]. Both BHA and BHT are currently permitted in pet food (and human food) at low levels in the US and in Europe.

Ethoxyquin (E324) was once a popular artificial antioxidant in pet food, but the use of this preservative was 'suspended' by the European Food Safety Authority in 2017 because of concerns about the side effects[12]. However, ethoxyquin is still widely used outside the EU.

Other artificial preservatives have been associated with cancer and cell damage and most people would agree that using artificial preservatives in food is not ideal, but it is better than consuming food that has decayed and which would make your dog ill. If you want the convenience of buying a long-lasting, dry dog food in large bags, it may be inevitable.

NATURAL PRESERVATIVES

Although artificial preservatives are less expensive and preserve food for longer, there has been a consumer-driven movement in recent years for high-end pet food manufacturers to use more natural preservatives. These preservatives come from plant sources and include tocopherols (vitamin E) from nuts and seeds, citric acid (vitamin C) from berries and tomatoes, and rosemary which contains antioxidants (rosmarinic acid and carnosic acid) to inhibit free radicals and help reduce the oxidization of fats and oils.

Although using plant extracts to preserve food may be more healthy than adding chemicals, it should be remembered that you will need to take more care of where foods preserved in this way are stored (making sure they are not exposed to damp or heat), as well as checking 'best before' dates on the packet. It may also be important to buy smaller bags so that there is less time for the food to be spoilt and for the fats to go rancid before your dog eats it.

As an alternative, canning and freezing food preserves it sufficiently for there to be no need to add any preservatives, providing, of course, there weren't any added to any of the individual ingredients before canning or freezing.

Colourings

Additives to provide colour to processed dog food include a range of naturally occurring food colours, food dyes or mineral-based colours. Common artificial colourings found in dog foods include:

- sunset yellow (E110/FD&C yellow 6)
- tartrazine (E102/FD&C yellow 5)
- ponceau 4r (E124/cochineal red A)
- patent blue V (E131)
- titanium dioxide (E171)

They may be listed by their E numbers or simply as 'colourings' on the label.

In humans, the use of artifical colourings in food has been linked to behavourial and health issues since the 1950s and more recent work has shown a clear link between food colourings and preservatives with hyperactivity in children[13]. No research has been done with dogs but there are anecdotal reports of owners noticing a big reduction in hyperactivity once highly coloured foods are removed from their diet.

It is worth remembering that dogs have a very powerful sense of smell many times greater and more nuanced than ours, but they do not have the same visual abilities as we do. While humans have three different types of cells in their eyes that allow them to see a wide range of colours, dogs have only two, allowing them to see in the blue and yellow spectrum only[14,15]. Dog food does therefore not need to be visually appealing (although the owners who buy it may prefer it to be). It is a sobering thought that chemical colours may be added for the benefit of humans rather than dogs. Dogs do not really care what food looks like, only whether it smells and tastes good.

Carbohydrates

Simple carbohydrates, found in sugar, honey and fruits, are easily and quickly broken down into glucose, which is absorbed into the blood stream and used as energy. Complex carbohydrates can be grouped into two further categories: starches and fibre. Starches are found in cereal grains and in starchy vegetables, such as potatoes and peas, and they take a bit longer to break down into glucose than simple carbohydrates. Fibre is any carbohydrate that isn't soluble and often passes out of the gut undigested.

In the human diet, an excess of grain carbohydrate (starch) and sugary foods is often blamed for high long-term insulin production in the body and associated with obesity and Type-2 diabetes, and many people have turned to Paleo-style diets in recent years where carbs are eliminated or reduced. But what is the truth of the situation when it comes to feeding our dogs?

Interestingly, most dogs have absolutely no need for the carbohydrates that come from grains or sugars in their diet – these carbs are not needed as part of the canine balanced diet. Some starches may be useful for some dogs with special dietary needs, such as a dog with pancreatitis or for others who use a huge amount of energy every day, but most pet dogs can get all the energy they need from eating protein and fats.

Evidence for this comes from groups of eminent scientists in both Europe and the USA who produce the guidelines for pet food manufacturers. The European pet food industry's governing body,

FEDIAF, produces the *FEDIAF Nutritional Guidelines for Complete and Complementary Pet Food for Cats and Dogs*. This is a comprehensive review of all current scientific studies produced as a practical guide for manufacturers and contains no mention of the need to feed carbohydrate to dogs. The guidelines are peer reviewed by independent veterinary nutritionists throughout Europe.

The report published by the American National Research Council of the National Academies – *Nutrient Requirements of Dogs and Cats* – provides nutrient recommendations based on physical activity and stages in life and explicitly declares that carbohydrates are not a necessary part of an optimal canine diet: 'Thus, there appears to be no requirement for digestible carbohydrate in dogs provided enough protein is given to supply the precursors for glucogenesis'.

This doesn't mean dogs cannot utilize carbohydrate and, indeed, it has been a big part of many processed foods for many years. One study even suggests that dogs have evolved a genetic make-up better suited to utilizing cooked starch[16]. However, an ability to digest starch is very different from the ability to thrive on a predominantly starchy diet.

CARBS IN DOG FOOD

For many years, dog food manufacturers have been putting grains from cereals (such as wheat and rice) into their products – 40–60 per cent of the foods made by large commercial dog food manufacturers consist of this type of carbohydrate. Protein and fat from meat sources are a lot more expensive than cereals and lower costs mean more profits for the manufacturer. The cynical among us may think that this is the main reason for including such large amounts of grain and cereal carbohydrate without any thought to the consequences of the health of the dogs they feed.

Evidence for causing harm by feeding dogs on a diet consisting of large amounts of grain carbohydrate is only just being gathered. For example, it is suspected that kibble-based, carb-rich diets, rather than cleaning teeth, facilitate the build-up of unhealthy mouth microbes in the dog, leading to periodontal disease. A high-grain carb diet has also been implicated in flatulence, smelly coat and skin issues, and in weight gain and obesity. We know that overweight and obese dogs live up to 2 years less than dogs of the correct weight[17]. No one really knows for certain yet, but a diet with large amounts of this type of carbohydrate could be shortening our dogs' lives and costing owners more money at the vets.

As consumers become more educated and more owners become concerned about what they feed their dogs, dog foods have sprung up that are labelled as 'grain-free'. Careful examination of the labels, however, shows that other starches are being used instead, such as sweet potato, tapioca or peas. In some cases, these products contain just as much carbohydrate as those containing cereals. Although an association isn't proven yet, there have been some recent concerns about diets rich in these 'grain-free' starches and the incidence of heart disease DVM (dilated cardio-myopathy).

There is no legal requirement for manufacturers to list the amount of carbohydrate on dog food labels, although NFE (nitrogen-free extract) – another name for carbohydrate – may be listed. However, if this is missing and you want to work it out, the percentage of carbohydrate equals 100 minus the percentages of protein, fat, moisture and ash. (If the percentage of moisture is not listed on the label, assume it is 10 per cent since it has to be listed if it is over 14 per cent).

$$\text{\% carbohydrate} = 100 - (\text{\% protein} + \text{\% fat} + \text{\% moisture} + \text{\% ash})$$

When choosing a dog food, be aware of the amount of carbohydrate – whether in the form of cereal or other sugars or starches – and think about the impact it might have on your dog. All dogs are different and have their own requirements so take time to carefully choose what you feed your dog and read the labels. If you don't, you risk feeding your dog unnecessary cereals or other starches without realizing it, which may put your dog's long-term health in danger.

A dog-friendly diet

Just like us, dogs thrive on a diet of fresh healthy ingredients. In recent years, there has been a move away from processed convenience foods towards diets that are prepared at home, in both human and canine diets. As dog-owners have begun to pay more attention to their own diets, there has been an increasing demand for a more natural way to feed our pets and a large number of companies have begun to offer more 'natural' food for dogs.

If you want to prepare your dog's food yourself, you will need to make sure its nutritional content is adequate, which requires dedication to reading and learning from many different sources to get a balanced approach. If you do not have time to do this yourself, a range of small dog food companies now cater for this market and many pet food shops and chains have freezer cabinets where a whole range of meat products are available that are perfectly balanced and 'complete' according to pet food industry standards. It is even possible to have good-quality frozen food delivered to your door for a relatively low cost. This makes it easy to feed your dog a wholesome fresh diet without the need to worry about whether the food you are providing your dog is complete and balanced. This is the best way to start fresh or raw-food feeding.

RAW AND FRESHLY PREPARED DIETS

Some dog owners have started moving towards the practice of raw feeding or preparing their dog's food themselves on the basis that it is more 'natural' and more nutritious. Preparing your dog's food also means you can have a direct influence on what your dog is eating. There are advocates for and opponents against this approach and it takes courage and a genuine desire to do the right thing for your dog to make the move away from feeding practices that have been established for decades. However, there may be genuine reasons for doing so.

One of the most important reasons is that you can see and smell what your dog is eating, ensuring that the ingredients are both fresh and nutritious. You will know that it hasn't been cooked at high temperatures and pressures and so it retains all of its vital nutrients. You will know that the food doesn't contain additives and your dog's diet will not be full of carbohydrates that they do not need and which may cause weight gain. In addition, if the meat and other ingredients are fresh when frozen, you can thaw and feed without any degradation of the fats and other components, and the raw ingredients will also contain plenty of beneficial microorganisms to provide variety to your dog's microbiota helping protect your dog from disease.

Further benefits of a raw or freshly prepared diet include better health, a stronger immune system, a shiny coat, smaller firmer stools, no unpleasant flatulence, the smell-free odour of a naturally fed dog, self-emptying anal glands, and cleaner teeth.

RAW DIET = HAPPY DOG

There is also a newly emerging link between serotonin production (the hormone that helps regulate mood and keeps us happy) and a beneficial microbiota in the gut[18,19]. Germ-free mice, for example, produce up to 60 per cent less serotonin than mice with conventional bacteria in their guts. If a healthy gut makes a happy dog, and one of the key components is a healthy microbiota, it makes sense to feed a raw meat-based diet which has been shown to promote a more balanced growth of bacterial communities and more diversity.

There is also good evidence that, given a choice, dogs choose high-protein meals over high-carbohydrate food every time. Giving them a diet that is raw or freshly prepared and high in protein rather than a high-carbohydrate, kibble-based diet is likely to be their preferred option[20].

Switching between different brands of processed food needs to be done slowly, with the new food being gradually introduced to avoid upsetting the digestion. In comparison, raw food is more natural for their digestive processes so ill effects are rarely seen if a rapid switchover takes place. However, to be on the safe side, a gradual transition using one quarter of the new food for a few days before progression to half and so on may be beneficial.

IS IT SAFE TO FEED MEAT RAW?

All raw meat will contain microorganisms with the potential to cause disease, but the extent depends on where in the carcass the meat came from, how fresh it is, and how it has been stored. This is no different to meat prepared in your kitchen for human consumption and good food hygiene principles need to be applied to ensure safety for both humans and dogs. Particular care is needed in a household with young children, pregnant women, those with a weakened immune system and older adults, but this also applies to all pet foods, not just raw.

Carnivores can tolerate eating more bacteria than humans because of the amount of acid in their stomachs, which is about ten times more than in non-carnivores. Their shorter guts also make for quick passage of the food, so there is no time for rotting[21]. If, however, you do not want to feed raw food to your dog, it is possible to lightly cook it instead, but be aware that this may do some damage to the nutrients it contains[22].

There is a risk that raw meat will contain pathogens such as *Salmonella* and *Campylobacter* and other parasites which can affect humans as well as

dogs. However, most of these pathogens are killed by freezing the meat for just three weeks at −20°C or colder[23,24]. The exception is *Salmonella*. In Europe, there is a zero-tolerance policy towards *Salmonella* and very stringent control systems are enforced by an inspectorate system for both human and animal food. In other parts of the world, systems may not be so stringent and so *Salmonella* contamination needs to be controlled by carefully choosing where you buy your meat and by rigorous hygiene routines.

As a general rule, the more you pay for the meat you feed to your dog, the better quality it will be.

If you buy minced meat products, remember that mincing not only disguises the appearance of the original cuts to some extent, but it also provides more surface area for bacteria to breed and so very careful sourcing and storage is needed. If possible, find a source of unminced meat offcuts and let your dog's teeth and stomach do the mincing. Finding a reputable business to supply you with good-quality fresh meat and bones at a reasonable cost is essential if you want your dog to eat raw food.

WHAT TO FEED

A freshly prepared diet needs to contain approximately:

40% meat, with some fish (including approximately 10% organ meat)

Appropriate muscle meats: chicken, turkey, rabbit, lamb, duck, venison, zebra, kangaroo, game, fish and tripe.

Organ meats (avoid mincing because of the risk of increased bacteria): heart, kidney, liver, pancreas and tripe.

40% meaty bones (with the bones themselves constituting approximately 10%)

Bones (raw, never cooked): non-weight-bearing bones, such as chicken and turkey wings, necks and backs, rib bones and any soft or spongy bone that can be chewed and eaten without splintering (see page 84).

20% mixture of pulverized vegetables, fruit, berries, nuts, herbs and seeds

These need to be blended to ensure that cell walls are crushed, allowing nutrients to become accessible. Make a thick raw soup from fresh ingredients every day or every few days and try to include as many colours and varieties as possible. It makes sense to use whatever is locally grown and seasonal. Some dogs don't really enjoy eating this part of their diet but it is an important source of all the vitamins and minerals they need. Mixing it in with the meat portion or hiding it in pockets of muscle meat may be necessary.

In addition, you should provide a source of fresh omega 3 fats as well as some additional minerals and vitamins. Feed your dog oily fish once a week, either fresh (raw) or from a can. Canning does not destroy the quality of either EPA or DHA (the fatty acids found in fish), so ethically sourced tinned sardines or mackerel are a convenient way to provide this part of their nutritional requirement[25].

Whatever you choose to feed your dog by way of fresh ingredients, remember that variety is key to ensuring all of the necessary food groups and nutrients are fed in the correct amounts. Choose different options whenever possible rather than sticking to a rigid formula that may not contain all the nutrients your dog needs in their diet.

There is the additional possibility that foods may not contain the amounts of vitamins and minerals they once did. Intensive farming and long transportation times may adversely affect the quality of foods, so it is wise to add a daily supplement that contains vitamins and minerals specially formulated for dogs.

For more on this, read authors such as Nick Thompson, Karen Becker, Steve Brown, Ian Billinhurst, Tom Lonsdale and Wendy Volhardt.

PROCESSED DIET

ADVANTAGES	DISADVANTAGES
✔ convenient, can seem easier if new to dog owning	✘ can contain high proportion of carbohydrate that can lead to weight gain and obesity
✔ has become 'normal' and so thought to be safe	✘ you can't see what goes into the food
✔ can seem low cost	✘ difficult to make judgments on the quality of protein in the food
✔ often will have your vet's support and they may sell processed foods	✘ can contain preservatives
	✘ can contain other additives such as artificial colours
	✘ high temperatures and pressures needed to create pellets can denature vital nutrients
	✘ you will need to clean your dog's teeth or cope with periodontal disease
	✘ your dog may have flatulence and may have a 'doggy odour'
	✘ lack beneficial effects on gut microbiota

RAW/FRESHLY PREPARED DIET

ADVANTAGES	DISADVANTAGES
✔ you can see and smell what is going into the food and so guarantee that all ingredients are fresh and wholesome	✘ not as convenient as processed food
✔ no preservatives are needed	✘ can appear to be more costly if you buy high-quality ingredients*
✔ your dog's teeth will stay clean and free of periodontal disease	✘ it is harder to know what to feed and you need to be informed in order to make sure your dog's diet is balanced and complete
✔ faeces are smaller and better formed so are easy to pick up	✘ you may need freezer storage
✔ anal glands are less likely to need emptying due to firmer stools	✘ your vet may raise objections if they are not yet familiar with all aspects this feeding practice
✔ your dog's coat and skin will be healthier	
✔ increases the diversity of gut microbiota, so your dog's immune system is stronger	
✔ flatulence is rare	
✔ no carbohydrate makes it easier to keep your dog at a healthy weight	

*Although good-quality raw food may cost more, it will be better quality and will not contain carbohydrate that your dog's body does not need. Since your dog is likely to be healthier as a result of eating high-quality food, you are likely like to be paying out less for veterinary fees in the long run.

Storage

All food spoils over time and when it's exposed to the environment. This decay results in the loss of essential nutrients and the possible introduction of diseases. Therefore, just as with human food, all the food your dog eats should be as fresh as possible.

If you are feeding your dog dry food, it's important to store it properly because it will decay rapidly once the bag is opened – fats will oxidize, the nutrients will degrade and the food may become infested with moulds, mites and other spoilers. The 'best if used by' date applies only to unopened bags (an intact bag with no holes or tears). Use dry food in an opened packet within seven days, buying smaller bags if you need to in order to use them up within this time. Buy recently produced food (check the date of production on the packet) and store it, once opened, in the original packaging in an airtight container in a dry place. A kitchen cupboard is much better than in an outhouse or similar. If the food smells rancid or your dog refuses to eat it, throw it away[26].

Even when food is frozen, it can be contaminated by oxygen, turning the fats rancid and slowly degrading the vitamins and antioxidants. Nutrients and fish oils are further degraded by ice crystals. If feeding frozen foods, buy only recently frozen foods (or freeze fresh foods yourself) and use within three months if possible. Use a rotation system in your freezer so all foods are used in order of purchase. Whole meats have a longer freezer life than minced meats or offal, and can be stored for longer, but keeping to a three-month schedule for everything will make things easy and ensure that the quality of foods is preserved[27].

Dairy

It is not necessary to feed dairy products as part of a balanced diet for dogs and some dogs are even lactose intolerant, as humans are. Any food containing lactose can make these dogs very unwell. For other dogs, some might enjoy small pieces of cheese as training treats but there is otherwise no need to include dairy products in their diet.

Vegetarian dog food

While dogs will happily exist on a vegetarian diet (and there are some commercially available), we do not know what the long-term consequences of a lifetime's consumption will be or whether it has an effect on a dog's health or longevity. Humans are omnivores and vegetarianism and veganism can be their choice, but given what we know about a dog's propensity to be carnivorous, it is likely that there may be consequences to feeding a meat-free diet. The truth is that we just do not know for certain. Until we find out, it may be best to avoid feeding your dog a meat-free diet.

Diet for the individual

Just as with humans, every dog is an individual and a diet that suits one dog's body may not suit another. Being sensitive to your dog's needs and informed about what you choose to feed will result in the best chance for your dog to be healthy and happy.

Dogs require different foods and differing quantities of food depending on whether they are neutered, producing puppies, at different life stages and whether they are more, or less, active. Different breeds may thrive on different foods, although there is no research to support this idea at present, and some dogs will have allergies to food or intolerances that you will need to take into consideration.

Finding the right diet can seem daunting for a first-time dog owner as there is so much choice and so much controversy about what is best. It is important to be well informed so you can make an intelligent choice and not be pressured into doing anything other than what you think is best for your dog. Given how important food is to health and longevity, it is worth taking time and effort to find what really works for your dog as an individual and to be flexible as they go through life's changes.

A messy issue

One of the more unpleasant duties that dog owners have to perform is picking up and disposing of our dogs' poop. Although this is not pleasant to do, it does give you a daily or twice daily opportunity to check on the health of your dog's digestive system.

Ideally, for your sake and your dog's, faeces should be easy to pick up. Freshly prepared and raw diets usually result in faeces that are fully formed, firm and small, providing, of course, that your dog is in good health. These are easy to pick up with a bag ready for disposal.

Very hard white faeces could mean your dog is eating too much bone which can cause constipation. Carbohydrate-rich diets tend to produce smellier and softer faeces that are more difficult to pick up. Dribbles, liquid, bad smells, or runny blancmange-type faeces can be a sign of poor health or food intolerances and so a trip to the vet is needed.

How much to feed and a good weight

One of the best things you can do for your dog is to manage their weight – there is much scientific evidence that obesity in dogs has a significant adverse effect on their health and welfare. Overweight or obese dogs are likely to have a shorter lifespan[28,29], a poorer quality of life[30] and an increased risk of cancer, as well as various related diseases and disorders[31,32,33] (such as breathing difficulties, heart failure and diabetes) so it is important to be careful about the amount of calories your dog is consuming. Dogs will be happier and healthier, and will also live longer, if they are fed fewer calories rather than too many[34].

Some dogs, particularly those of certain breeds or dogs that have been neutered, often want to put on more weight than is good for them. Just like us, all dogs will get fat if they are eating too much of the wrong type of food, especially if carbohydrates and stress are involved. If your dog is already obese, it is important to get help from your veterinary surgery to slowly bring your dog's weight under control.

WSAVA Global Nutrition Committee

Body Condition Score

UNDER IDEAL

1. Ribs, lumbar vertebrae, pelvic bones and all bony prominences evident from a distance. No discernable body fat. Obvious loss of muscle mass.

2. Ribs, lumbar vertebrae, pelvic bones easily visible. No palpable fat. Some evidence of other bony prominences. Minimal loss of muscle mass.

3. Ribs easily palpated and may be visible with no palpable fat. Tops of lumbar vertebrae visible. Pelvic bones becoming prominent. Obvious waist and abdominal tuck.

IDEAL

4. Ribs easily palpable, with minimal fat covering. Waist easily noted, viewed from above. Abdominal tuck evident.

5. Ribs palpable without excess fat covering. Waist observed behind ribs when viewed from above. Abdomen tucked up when viewed from the side.

OVER IDEAL

6. Ribs palpable with slight excess fat covering. Waist is discernable viewed from above but is not prominent. Abdominal tuck is apparent.

7. Ribs palpable with difficulty; heavy fat cover. Noticeable fat deposits over lumbar area and base of tail. Waist absent or barely visible. Abdominal tuck may be present.

8. Ribs not palpable under very heavy fat cover, or palpable only with significant pressure. Heavy fat deposits over lumbar area and base of tail. Waist absent. No abdominal tuck. Obvious abdominal distention may be present.

9. Massive fat deposits over thorax, spine and base of tail. Waist and abdominal tuck absent. Fat deposits on neck and limbs. Obvious abdominal distention.

wsava.org

To decide whether your dog is a healthy weight or not, the World Small Animal Veterinary Association Global Nutrition Panel recommend the body condition score (BCS) scale in dogs (as pictured, left) since it has been the most extensively validated. The ideal score is 5, dogs with a BCS of 6 or 7 are 'overweight', while those with a BCS of 8 or 9 are classified as having obesity, which is equivalent to at least 30 per cent excess weight.

Some dogs become overweight because owners stick rigorously to the top end of guides provided by manufacturers on dog food packaging, while others give appropriate amounts of food but then provide a large number of calories in the form of treats and snacks. Carbohydrate-rich diets and snacks containing poor-quality protein and fats could also be a major cause of overeating since a dog will try to eat more to provide itself with adequate nutrition.

Some owners find it difficult to put their pets on a diet, feeling it is unkind to withhold food when their dog is asking for it, especially at human mealtimes. But those same owners would not dream of deliberately withholding medication needed to keep their dog alive or refusing to take their dog to a veterinary hospital for surgery if it was necessary. If you have an overweight or obese dog, think of it as a medical emergency to help you to harden your heart and not give extra treats or bowls of food. Dogs are very adaptable and if the rules about feeding change and are consistent, it doesn't take them more than a few days to get into a new routine. When you feel the need to give your dog extra treats or food, take them for a little play in the garden or do something more interesting instead to take both your minds off food.

TRAINING TREATS

A treat needs to be something your dog will enjoy and consider worth working for, whether it's for coming to you in the park when called, for getting into the car or just settling down beside you while you rest.

A dog's preference is for meat – preferably a warm, moist piece of cooked muscle meat. Many people use chopped and slow-cooked liver baked at a low temperature and while this makes a delicious treat that many dogs consider very high value, it can make the house smell extremely unpleasant during cooking! If you have the time, cook and chop up muscle meat into small pieces to make ideal dog-friendly treats. Very small pieces of dried lamb or beef tripe (which has its own rich smell, even when dried!) also make very acceptable treats.

Biscuits made of cereals just don't have the same appeal, so if you want your treats to be effective, they need to have a high meat content and not be too dry so your dog can smell them from afar.

It is possible to find shop-bought training treats with a high meat content and few or no additives, colourings or preservatives. Make sure you store these treats as you would any fresh meat product. It is also possible for dogs to enjoy cereal-based treats if they are coated in fats and meat digest to disguise their content. Although dogs will often find these treats acceptable, I wouldn't recommend them as you should consider whether you should be 'tricking' your dog into eating these treats that they normally would not be interested in if not for the coating. Check the ingredients list on the labels of any shop-bought treats in exactly the same way that you would a food packaging label (see page 54).

Beware of treats containing ingredients to which your dog may be intolerant or allergic. Unless the treat is pure meat, always start with low quantities of a new treat at first and gradually build up to avoid an unsettled digestion. Just like us, dogs can lose interest if they are fed the same treats on a regular basis, so provide some variety to keep interest levels high. Remember to take the extra calories into account if you are feeding a lot of treats and consider the unbalancing effect on your dog's diet.

POISONOUS HUMAN FOOD

Some human foods are poisonous to dogs, so it is essential to keep your dog away them. Those that would be toxic to dogs in the quantities they would be found in a normal home include:

- Grapes and their dried equivalents (raisins, sultanas and so on)
- Chocolate – especially those with a high cocoa solids content
- Xylitol and all cakes/biscuits/peanut butter and so on made with this artificial sweetener
- Macadamia nuts
- Onions
- Garlic in excess

Chewing and dental health

Not only is living with a dog with evil-smelling breath unpleasant for us, it will be uncomfortable and ultimately painful for the dog, potentially toxic to their bodies and possibly life-threatening.

Food, especially sticky food containing high levels of grain carbohydrates or sugar, accumulates along your dog's gumline to form bacteria-laden plaque on teeth. This happens in just a few weeks and, if not removed, it transforms over time into hard tartar (also called calculus) which irritates the gums and leads to gingivitis (reddening of the gums bordering the teeth). Eventually spaces form between the teeth and gums, allowing bacteria in, and can lead to tissue destruction and bone loss in just 6 months[35] which will, eventually, lead to tooth loss.

During this process, your dog will have smelly breath, will feel uncomfortable and eventually have a painful mouth, and may be reluctant to eat or chew. The bacteria growing in the mouth will also overwork the immune system and make it harder for the dog to fight other diseases or infections. Eventually, an operation, possibly several, with the associated life-threatening risks, will be necessary to remove the tartar build-up, clean up the gums and remove any loose teeth. Periodontal disease is particularly likely in tiny dogs that usually have crowded mouths.

Dogs that are fed dried and canned meats, which do not control plaque formation as they are not sufficiently abrasive to keep the teeth clean, should have their teeth cleaned daily to stop the build-up of plaque. Many owners either don't have time or find doing it a chore and so leave long gaps in between brushing thereby making it ineffective, so harnessing your dog's natural desire to chew and providing chews and foods that are natural tooth cleaners may be a better and easier solution.

Many dogs love to chew, especially puppies and young dogs, and may steal household items such as shoes and the TV remote if not given more appropriate items. Providing safe items to chew and gnaw on while puppies are teething and during the adolescent chewing phase (usually 7–12 months) leads to a lifetime chewing habit which will help keep teeth clean and mouths healthy long into old age. Chewing and gnawing is a natural behaviour that dogs enjoy, so you can also provide hours of happy contentment if you give your dog appropriate items that it will enjoy chewing.

SUPERVISED CHEWING

Safety is important. There is always a risk when your dog is chewing that it will swallow a bulky or dangerous item or something may get stuck in its gullet or mouth. Allowing dogs to chew a wide variety of appropriate items will help them build good skills at manipulating objects and they are less likely to try to swallow them whole or get them stuck. In particular, give inexperienced dogs very large chews so they can't swallow them whole. (See page 86.)

Always supervise your dog when it is chewing so you can help if any difficulties arise, make sure they don't chew or eat faster than is good for them, or try to swallow it whole. Try not to get too close, though, particularly if you have a possessive dog.

Try to provide two different types of chew each day, taking away anything remaining at the end of the day and giving two new chews the next day. As well as helping to keep their teeth clean, your dog will be occupied and interested and less likely to chew inappropriate and possibly dangerous or expensive household items.

Some chews, particularly meaty bones, will be highly prized by your dog and you will need a strategy for getting them back if you need to stop your dog chewing quickly. Things that may work are producing your dog's lead and offering a walk (don't disappoint or it won't work next time), rattling the treat tin,

ringing the doorbell and pretending there is someone there or, if you know your dog is not possessive, carefully offer something more tempting and lure your dog out of the room or garden before feeding the new treat so you can shut the door and pick up the chew in your own time. Alternatively, give chews half an hour before dinner, and then remove the chews while your dog is eating.

Chewing bones

There is much controversy over whether to feed bones or not with vociferous veterinary surgeons giving their opinions from both side of the fence. It is up to you whether you feed your dog bones or not and you do this at your own risk, but here is the information you should know before you do.

The wrong type of bone or bones, or feeding bones in the wrong way, can cause impactions, perforations and obstructions of the gut. However, it is perfectly possible to safely feed bones to dogs if you are careful and many people do so on a daily basis. Bones are a very small percentage of items regularly pulled out of dogs' digestive tracts by veterinary surgeons[36]. Bones and any meat attached are great natural tooth cleaners and can even help to remove tartar once it has formed[37].

Bones can be divided into those fed as part of a natural, or raw feeding, diet and recreational bones, given to dogs to provide interest and to help keep their teeth clean. Those that are part of the diet are usually soft and easily crushed by a dog's jaws, such as ribs, or poultry backs, wings and necks.

Recreational bones are usually the large limb bones of more mature meat animals (those of older livestock which are often sold to make soups or stock) and are usually the harder weight-bearing bones. These bones can cause occasional dental damage, especially if you give your dog a sawn bone, and large pieces too hard to be digested can break off, so do not give this type of bone to novice dogs in their first year of bone eating.

ALL bones should be fed raw. Never feed cooked bones of any sort as these can splinter and the sharp edges can tear the intestine.

When you start feeding bones, it is best to start small and gradually build up to prevent your dog chewing up large amounts or trying to ingest lots of bone without chewing properly. It may be best to start with a few chicken wings daily and gradually build up to a small number of ribs or a trachea.

BONE HYGIENE

Hygiene is important when feeding bones, so follow this best practice:

- Train your dog to stay on a mat or towel that you can wash afterwards, or confine your dog in such a way that the floor area can be cleaned well. Alternatively, feed bones in the garden and do not let your dog bring them inside.
- As soon as your dog has walked away from the bone, remove it to a container and keep it in the fridge.
- Do not leave bones in the garden – they will attract snails which are a vector for lungworm.
- Throw the bone away if it starts to smell.
- If your dog has long ears or long hair, tuck them into a snood or soft scarf beforehand to keep everything clean. If this is not possible, a face/beard/ear/paw wash after chewing may be necessary.

If you have more than one dog, make sure you feed each dog in a separate room or area and don't allow them back together until all remaining bones have been picked up and put away. This will avoid any competition over bones and will also stop dogs from

trying to eat their bones as quickly as possible to keep it from others.

For similar reasons, it is best not to interfere with your dog during bone chewing. Any staring or hovering could make them eat too fast or may provoke possessiveness. It is better to leave them alone but to supervise discretely from a distance.

Chews

There is a huge variety of dog chews on the market. Avoid anything inedible such as plastic toys or rubber bones – chews should be made of something that can be digested, even though they take a long time to eat.

Good chews to seek out are any parts of a meat animal that have been air dried, including skin (also known as jerky), fish skin, chicken or duck feet or bills, antlers (soft bone), noses, ears and hooves. These don't sound very appealing, and you may not want to have them on the floor when sensitive friends are due to visit, but they are very good for dogs and they will keep your dog occupied and naturally fulfilled for some time.

Processed rawhide (skin) may look clean and inviting but it has usually been treated with dubious chemicals which make it slippery and rubbery when chewed. You can also buy chews made with cereals, often also containing milk, which are quickly eaten and more like a snack than a chew. As always, read the label and find out the ingredients and number of calories before feeding.

STRANGE CRAVINGS

Some dogs like to eat items that are not edible, such as stones, toys, items of clothing and so on. This disorder – an appetite for something that is inedible and has no nutritional value – is known as 'pica'. This behaviour can be very harmful and requires immediate attention.

Sometimes dogs will swallow items to prevent their owners getting hold of them. Some dogs will gnaw on stones as if trying to get nourishment. Another unpleasant eating habit is eating faeces (coprophagia), sometimes their own, sometimes other dogs', or perhaps that of cats or foxes.

Pica and coprophagia are common among dogs and you should not be embarrassed about talking to your vet. The first step in their treatment is to determine if they are caused by a dietary deficiency or a bad habit, so the best place to start investigating strange cravings is your veterinary practice.

CHAPTER 4

Hydration

A worried owner called with an unusual question: 'How do I stop my two rescue Weimaraners fighting over an empty water dish?'.

These two-year-old brothers would happily eat out of separate metal dishes next to each other but would start to get cross if they came across their water dish at the same time. After doing some digging into the records left with the rescue organization when the previous owners had given them up, we discovered these Weimaraners had grown up in a back garden. Their body condition had been good on arrival at the rescue centre, and they came with beds, bowls and a bag of dry food, so they hadn't been neglected. Further testing revealed that these dogs would only get upset with each other over an empty water dish or one with a few drops left in the bottom. We could only guess that their water dish had only been filled up sporadically and that these brothers had learned that water was a scarce resource worth them having such fights over.

Water is essential for your dog to stay healthy since it is involved in all bodily processes, from digesting food to removing toxins. To keep your dog on top form, they must have access to good-quality water at all times. Even a healthy dog will struggle to live without water for more than a few days and repeated periods of drought will cause problems with their kidneys and other organs.

It is usual, in most households, for water to be constantly available. However, since dogs are restricted by our lifestyles, fences and leashes and cannot find water themselves, we must remember to provide all they need. It is really just a matter of remembering to refill and refresh the water dish on a regular basis, but some owners find this easier than others. If you are great at routines, making water bowl washing and filling part of your daily ritual ensures fresh clean water is always available for your dog. Keep the bowl in view in the kitchen to remind you, rather than tucked away somewhere it is rarely seen. Many a dry water bowl has been missed because it was hidden behind a door or in another room. Use a large, flat-bottomed bowl so that it is less easily knocked over and, if you forget to fill it one day, there will still be residual water from the previous day. It may not be fresh but at least it's available and will prevent your dog from going thirsty. If you are not great at daily routines, try setting a daily electronic alarm.

Not only is staying hydrated better for dogs' bodies, the urine of a reluctant drinker is more concentrated and therefore more toxic to grass. Providing good-quality water at all times could help to prevent your lawn from developing brown patches.

Water quality

Why is it that dogs often seem to prefer to drink out of the toilet bowl or muddy puddles rather than from their nice clean bowl? Dogs have the nasal apparatus, neurons and sufficient smell-processing power in their brains to smell one teaspoon of sugar dissolved in two Olympic-size swimming pools[1] (see page 205). Perhaps you washed the bowl with a soapy cloth and didn't rinse, or the dishwasher left a residue? Or the cloth had bleach or other harmful cleaning products that got passed onto the bowl. Or sometimes it's the water itself. Tap water is usually purified with chlorine or other agents that even we can detect at normal concentrations, so imagine how strong this might smell to a dog. Chlorine diffuses out of water if it's left long enough, which is perhaps why water in a toilet bowl may be more attractive.

Filtering water removes chlorine and, in my experience, dogs will drink a lot more if given access to filtered water rather than water straight from the tap. Providing water that your dog likes to drink may seem unimportant, and filtering water for your dog may seem time-consuming, but with their special senses for chemical detection, this simple act could make the difference between them being happily hydrated and only drinking when there is a real need. Be sure to double rinse the bowl too to reduce the risk of contamination from cleaning materials.

Leaving a bowl outside to collect rainwater may seem like a sensible option but, unfortunately, it may be impossible to prevent rats and other animals from using it too. These creatures may carry and pass on diseases such as Leptospirosis, which dogs can catch, so it's not advisable to do this.

Dry food and hydration

Remember that if you feed your dog kibble, which has been dehydrated, the food will either need to be soaked beforehand or your dog will need to drink a lot of water once the dry food reaches its stomach. Feeding dry food often results in a dog overdrinking and the excess water will then need to be excreted. Apart from making their kidneys work harder, this could mean that your dog needs to go to the toilet at a time that isn't convenient. If you feed your dog late in the evening and then shut it away for the night, or feed first thing in the morning and then go to work, it can mean your dog is uncomfortable and restless and can result in unwanted puddles on the floor.

Consider meal timings and soak dry food before feeding, or feed your dog an alternative diet (see page 64). Do watch out for signs of increased thirst that are not food related and consult a veterinarian as this could mean that your dog is ill.

Keeping cool

Dogs lose heat by panting – they use their lungs to blow air over the surface of the tongue which is kept moist with plenty of watery saliva; blood vessels in the tongue dilate, allowing the air to take out the heat and so cool the body. Lack of water can hinder this process and lead to dangerous overheating. Despite how good dogs are at losing heat via their tongues, no dog can cope if temperatures rise too high and every care needs to be taken to make sure they have shade on a very hot day and are not left inside cars on warm days.

Tube-shaped muzzles that restrict the mouth should only be used for brief periods and never when a dog is taking exercise or likely to be in a hot environment.

Just like humans, dogs need water to maintain their body temperature when it's hot, so it is essential to provide access to water when the sun is out or if your dog has thick fur. Don't forget to take water and a dish and provide plenty of drinking opportunities throughout the day if you take your dog away from home or on a long walk.

CHAPTER 5

Sex and neutering

You never really know what you are going to find when you enter someone's home to help with a dog behaviour problem.

Billy, a 10-month-old Beagle, was extremely friendly, if a little demanding, as I walked in. Eventually his owner and I sat down to talk and before we had even got started, Billy started a loud baying at a volume that rocked the room, looking directly at us as if daring us to try to hold a conversation without him. His female owner tried, unsuccessfully, to silence him and got up to chase him as he pulled away. Undeterred and tail waving, he jumped onto the sofa, pulled a large cushion onto the middle of the floor and proceeded to hump it vigorously. Face hidden behind her hands as she sat down, his exasperated owner said, 'this is another problem; we are going to get him castrated'.

Just at that moment, I heard the front door click and Billy ran to greet his male owner with loud resonating barks. 'Good boy, get down, quiet now,' I heard him say as he pushed his way into the room. 'Sorry I'm late,' he said, as he knelt down to recharge his mobile phone using the socket between the sofa and chair. For a moment he was in the head down/bottom up position and Billy took full advantage, clasping the back end of his owner and humping enthusiastically while his female owner looked on with increasing embarrassment. 'I'm so sorry', she said, 'he is always like this when we have visitors, especially when the grandchildren visit. He's obsessed. We have to get him done soon.'

Further conversations with the owners (with Billy temporarily confined to the kitchen with a tasty chew so we could talk uninterrupted) revealed that this dog had learned to be very good at getting his owners' attention, but had not learned to tone it down when they were busy or had guests. The humping was not because of rampant sexual urges, even though he was in peak adolescence. Instead it was just another, very effective way to get everyone's attention, especially during times of great excitement such as when visitors arrived and he was being ignored.

Billy didn't need castrating at all. He just needed to learn a different way to behave and his owners needed different strategies to manage him and use his energies in, shall we say, more productive ways.

So many dogs are neutered to affect a change in their behaviour when their behaviour has motivations that are not to do with the urge to reproduce. Other dogs are neutered because their owners consider it 'the thing to do' and are complying with a current social norm. But is it best for your particular dog's welfare and wellbeing? The choice you make on behalf of your dog in this regard can have a profound effect. It may seem 'normal' for your dog to be neutered, but it is not a 'natural' solution.

Sex hormones and timing

All dogs are individuals, but puberty usually happens around six months of age – slightly sooner in smaller dogs and slightly later in larger dogs. Sex hormones begin to be secreted within the body at puberty in both sexes to prepare the body for reproduction. As with human teenagers, adolescent dogs show a change in behaviour at this time and are likely to become much more focused on things in the outside world rather than home and their owners. You may experience a less close relationship, as well as control issues when out and your dog will be much less responsive to you, preferring, instead, to pay more attention to things outside the home. For owners experiencing this phase, it is important to remember that it is a natural life stage that will eventually pass. Adolescence ends with social maturity, which gradually arrives with more mature behaviour patterns. Most dogs are socially mature by about 18 months but it can be as soon as a year for small breeds whereas large dogs may take up to three years. Males are often slower to mature than females.

Neutering

In some places, such as Germany and Scandinavia, neutering (the surgical removal of the uterus and ovaries in a female or testes in a male) is considered

mutilation and it is governed by strict laws. In other parts of the world, neutering is considered a routine operation and a policy of neutering all dogs has become the norm.

Since we are only just discovering the effects neutering has on dogs, and evidence is slowly emerging that it may not be in an individual dog's best interests, a more considered approach might be better. Whether you decide to neuter or not is a decision you must take on your dog's behalf and it needs to be a fully informed one, not just something that has to be done because you feel a pressure to do so. Each case should be assessed on its own merits and with consideration for the individual dog and its family. Becoming informed requires that you dig out and assess all the available evidence, especially the new research since that might tell a different story to what

is currently known. Consider the following factors before you make a decision for your dog:

- What are the reasons for neutering?
- What are the consequences of keeping your dog entire?
- Will neutering definitely get rid of a behaviour problem?
- Are there any negative health consequences of neutering?
- Is neutering a good welfare decision for your individual dog?
- If you do decide to have your dog neutered, when is the best age to have it done?

Neutering for health – pros and cons

The following is not an exhaustive list but it gives you an idea of the scientific work that has been done to date and the complexity of the issue. It is intended as a place to start rather than a comprehensive guide since not every aspect has yet been studied and new information is constantly emerging.

CASTRATION (REMOVAL OF A MALE DOG'S TESTES)

PROS	CONS
✔ Prevents prostate and testicular problems[1,2,3,4]	✘ Urethral sphincter incontinence (uncommon)[5]
	✘ Musculoskeletal problems[6,7,8,9,10]
	✘ Obesity[11]
	✘ Cancer of the prostate, lymphocytes, urinary system, blood vessels and bones[12,13,14,15,16,17]
	✘ Autoimmune disease[18]
	✘ Adverse vaccine reaction[19]
	✘ Cognitive decline increase[20]

SPAYING
(REMOVAL OF THE OVARIES AND UTERUS OF A FEMALE DOG)

PROS	CONS
✔ Eliminates chance of pyometra (occurs in 23% of dogs before 10 years of age)[21]	✘ Urinary sphincter incontinence[25,26,27,28]
✔ Reduces risk of mammary cancer[22] (however, a systematic review[23] disputed this finding and found no convincing evidence that neutering reduces the risk)	✘ Cystitis if spayed before puberty[29,30]
✔ Eliminates risk of reproductive tract tumours[24] but risk is less than 0.5% for entire females	✘ Musculoskeletal problems[31,32,33,34,35,36]
✔ Stops the estrus (heat) cycle with its attendant mess and behaviour fluctuations	✘ Obesity[37,38]
	✘ Cancers of the lymphocytes, urinary system, blood vessels and bones[39,40,41,42,43,44,45,46]
	✘ Cognitive decline increase[47]
	✘ Autoimmune disease[48]
	✘ Adverse vaccine reaction[49]

Behaviour problems and neutering

There is some scientific evidence to suggest that neutering may lead to more behaviour issues than it solves[50]. Neutering will only solve a behaviour problem that is being driven by a strong desire to reproduce. Even then, behaviour learned while the dog was entire may continue after neutering. For example, take the case of a male dog who is routinely escaping from the back garden and running off. If this is driven by the desire to look for a mate, it may be stopped by neutering because removing the testes will remove the desire. However, the dog may be running away because it is bored at home and is looking for company or stimulation. Neutering will then have no effect. Either way, once the dog has found out how exciting it is to break free, neutering will not solve the problem as he will continue to do it.

The following table is very simplistic and it is not an exhaustive list, but gives you some idea of the complexity of the information you need before you can make the right decision for your dog. Few dogs have a simple behaviour problem and issues caused by a strong sexual desire may also be driven by other strong urges too. Consulting a professional animal behaviour counsellor will help you to determine the true cause of your dog's behaviour problem and help you decide the best way forward.

BEHAVIOUR PROBLEM	CAUSE OF PROBLEM	SOLVED BY NEUTERING
Running away	To find a mate	Yes
	To find a playmate	No
	To find fun	No
	To exercise	No
Fighting with other dogs	Competition over a mate	Yes
	Fear (biggest cause of problems with other dogs)	No
Separation issues	Wanting to get out to find a mate	Yes
	Afraid to be in the house alone	No
	Afraid of isolation	No
	Bored and in need of stimulation	No
Excessive urine marking	To advertise to mates and competitors	Yes
	Marking due to insecurity	No
Fighting with another dog in the household	If driven by sexual competition	Yes
	If driven by competition over other resources or the owner's attention	No
Boisterousness	Due to lack of exercise or stimulation	No

CHEMICAL CASTRATION

Drugs are now available that mimic the results of surgical castration in both male and female dogs and these can be used to 'test out' the effect before you make an irreversible decision. These can be very useful in cases where it is difficult to tell whether neutering may help with a behaviour problem in your dog or not.

CHAPTER 6

Cooperation and sensitive handling

As I went to put the collar on my young Vizsla, he twisted away, moving towards the back door, too excited at the prospect of going for a walk to stand still for long.

A few days previously, I had taken off his usual collar when I had bathed him and it had inexplicably disappeared before I had a chance to put it back on. Until I could replace it, his temporary collar was that of a much-loved departed dog with a slightly smaller neck. Fine for walks but a bit too tight to be left on for too long. Hence, we had a new daily ritual of collar fitting before he went for a walk.

As he spun away from me, my first thought was to follow him, to get the job done faster, leaning over him and swiftly putting it on as he focused on willing the door to open. Instead I waited, collar unbuckled and held out in my hands ready for him to put his neck into it. He reached the door and looked back over his shoulder, wondering, no doubt, why I was being so slow at my door-opening duties that morning. He saw me standing there with collar outstretched and I made every effort to encourage him to come towards me, calling gently, nodding my head while looking from him to the collar, stepping back a little. Not being a dog to stand still for long and with plenty of positivity between us, he came trotting forward. I moved the collar towards his neck and, again, he spun away, moving towards the door. After

several of these approaches, and once I had schooled myself to keep my hands still, he began to realize that for some reason I was rooted to the spot and, calming now that the prospect of dashing out of the door was off the table, he kept still long enough for me to be able to put on his collar. This calm behaviour was rewarded almost at once with freedom as I swiftly did up the buckle, opened the door and he rushed outside.

The next day, it was a similar story but this time it took fewer tries before he stood still. This continued for a few days and then, one day to my surprise he came straight into the outstretched collar, pushing his neck against it so that I almost dropped it, as if to say 'let's get this over with so we can get on with the walk'. He did the same every day after that.

On that first day, it might have been quicker and easier to hold him still while I put on his collar, as he has no fear of being restrained and that was certainly my inclination. However, by deciding to take a little bit of time for a few days, by being patient and giving him a choice in how to proceed, he is now a willing participant in this daily task and it gives us a moment of happy cooperation at the start of the day which sets the tone of our walk together.

The power of choice and control

Much of this chapter is about the right to choose. Giving your dog a choice about how and when they will be handled when caring for their body is very powerful and completely contradictory to ways that many dogs are treated. If you want your dog to have the best life possible, giving them a say in how and when procedures that maintain their bodies (such as nail clipping and coat detangling) are done is important – this choice develops trust and cooperation that will improve their wellbeing and lead to a happier life. The resulting lack of stress gives them the best chance of an optimal life as well as health advantages (see page 183).

There will, of course, be times when your dog needs to accept handling even when they would prefer it not to happen, such as when they need urgent veterinary care, and for those circumstances, it is good to desensitize your dog to restraint and being handled under duress.

For all other handling, it is better to give your dog a choice about whether to interact with you or another human or not. You will, of course, need to stack the odds in your favour so they comply, but it is so much better for everyone if you have a willing accomplice rather than one who is constantly made to do things against their will.

The perils of forced contact

Some dogs have had pleasant and frequent handling from birth and will be able to cope with forced handling from people. The majority of dogs, however, do not enjoy it and some will find it very difficult and stressful indeed. A few dogs may become so frightened that they will start to defend themselves with growling and aggression, and even if they decide they do not want to bite family members they will remain in conflict for the whole of the procedure, caught between family loyalty and self-defense.

Imagine what it must be like to live with creatures much larger than you who are not able to tell you what is about to happen, who repeatedly force you to endure strange procedures such as clipping off your

fur or cutting your nails. They may also randomly drip liquid drops into your sore eyes or ears or put cream on a painful skin wound. While all these actions seem very necessary and justifiable to us, they may seem like major impositions and unnecessary and frightening to your dog. Visits to the dentist are probably the nearest we ever come to this and some people become absolutely terrified of having their teeth attended to. Even then, we have a degree of choice about whether or not to visit the dentist and we understand it is for our own good in the long run. Dogs are not so lucky.

If you have a dog with a long fine coat, you will probably have to groom them thoroughly every day to prevent any tangles developing into large

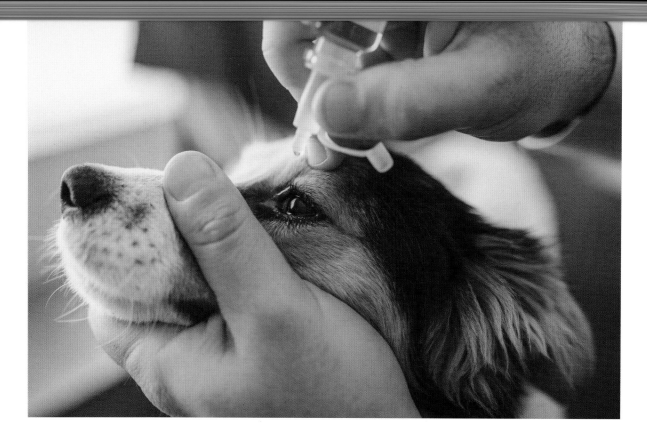

uncomfortable mats. For some dogs, having to submit to a daily procedure where your hair is tweaked and tugged painfully without any ability to ask for a break or for it to be done more gently can be really upsetting. Imagine having this happen to you every day, even on days where you are not feeling well, being reprimanded if you raise an objection, and being forced to endure the procedure for as long as your human wants to do it. It must be really confusing too. Most of the time an owner is really kind to them and nice to be around, but sometimes they do really unpleasant things and will not stop until they have decided they have done enough.

Unless your dog is a willing partner in routine body maintenance procedures, you can soon get to the point where your dog avoids you at certain times or when they spot the signals – like the shampoo bottle being taken out of a cupboard – that an assault on their person is likely. It will be damaging to your relationship for your dog to be always looking out

for these negative signals and it is not hard to see how this kind of random attack, from the dog's perspective, can ruin the trust between you and begin to erode the good relationship you have built up. Even if they just endure it with no aggressive repercussions, their stress levels will be through the roof every time an unpleasant event like this happens and repeated stressful events can have negative physical consequences (see page 183).

As well as being very stressful for your dog, this type of forced handling to get jobs done may also be unpleasant for you. This will be especially true if you behave positively to your dog most of the time and have a good relationship. You will know that your dog doesn't like what you are doing or is afraid, which could result in you putting off routine husbandry procedures that need to be done to maintain your dog's health and wellbeing. It is wise, therefore, to try to mitigate the effects of no-choice handling and avoid it altogether for daily or regular husbandry duties.

Touching, holding, hugging

As primates, we like to touch, hug and hold to show affection, but dogs do not generally touch, hold and hug each other unless they are fighting or mating (or playing). Consequently, our dogs need to get used to this from an early age. Some miss out on this opportunity and some may learn that human hands often grab them without sensitivity or may be used to punish them. It is beneficial for all pet dogs to learn that humans are capable of being kind and thoughtful when they touch. If you spend some time on this, any procedures necessary to care for their bodies will become much easier and they will learn to enjoy our primate ways of showing affection.

LEARNING ABOUT TOUCH

A good place to start is to help your dog learn to enjoy being touched all over. Observe what happens if you move slowly towards your dog with hands outstretched. Your goal is for your dog to move towards you and allow you to touch them all over, even in sensitive places like around the eyes or paws, with their body relaxed and soft with tail waving gently. Your dog may move towards you but tuck its tail underneath its body as you begin to touch, showing that they are not completely comfortable with what you might be about to do, or it may move away completely, indicating that you have a lot of ground to cover.

If this is the case, take every opportunity over the next few months to help your dog learn that human hands near its body is a good thing rather than bad. Start slowly by calling your dog to you and giving gentle soft touches in 'safe' areas, such as along the back and chest, gradually working up to more sensitive places such as under the tummy, head and paws. Make happy and encouraging noises when you start to do this to indicate that your intentions are positive and friendly.

Touch for a few seconds and then stop and observe. Is your dog's tail tucked under, ears back, body tense? Does your dog move away or stay close so you can do more? From your observations, it should be possible to decide if it is okay to continue or whether to leave it there and try again later. If your dog wants to move away, leave it and try again more gently and slowly next time.

Sensitive handling in this way will help your dog feel in control. Make a habit of doing this when both of you are relaxed to help your dog learn that human hands can bring pleasure and connection that feel good rather than scary. Work this up until your dog really enjoys a gentle full body massage and completely lets go of all muscle tension. During relaxed contact like this, oxytocin, the hormone known for its role in bonding, socialization and stress relief, is released into the bloodstream (of both you and your dog), bringing a deep feeling of happiness that will help to strengthen the bond between you as well as helping your dog to learn to enjoy the handling process[1].

While you are working on this, it is best to avoid any no-choice handling, always giving your dog the option to move away if they want to. Be patient and persistent about building the trust between you, particularly if your dog has had its trust damaged in the past by harsh handling from family members, previous owners, busy veterinary staff or a groomer who just wanted to get the job done as fast as possible. Some dogs will need time to learn to trust, but by doing this, you will be laying a good foundation for further work and will create an activity that will benefit your relationship and your respective stress levels.

HOW TO SENSITIVELY GREET YOUR DOG

When greeting your dog or calling your dog to you, try not to put your hands on their heads to pat or rub them. This is a very common practice by owners who want to show affection but, unfortunately, most dogs do not like it as it presses on their sensitive eyes, nose, ears and whiskers and so probably feels quite uncomfortable. Consequently, you will often see dogs move their heads away and shake or yawn, or try to avoid hands coming towards their heads by lifting their heads or by ducking and turning away. If this is your method of greeting, try instead to train yourself to touch them along the back or the chest, in less sensitive places, or be very gentle when you touch their heads and do not rub or pat.

How to give a choice

Once your dog is happy to be touched and stroked all over when both of you are in a relaxed state, it is time to work on attempting more intense handling of particular areas that may need to be seen to, such as legs, toes, paws, nails, eyes, mouth or ears. To find out where it is best to begin, run your hands over different parts of your dog's body and watch carefully for any signs of resistance. The signs may be very subtle, such as a slight leaning away or a tensing of the muscles or a slight lowering of the tail – notice every tiny movement your dog makes. Some breeds, such as Akitas or Rottweilers, are not good at showing their emotions or their discomfort so watch them very carefully. Make a list of the places on your dog's body in order of least concern and start at the top of this list, working on one area every day until your dog is completely comfortable about being touched there before moving on to the next.

Put a dish of tasty treats (real meat treats rather than cereal-based foods) on the side just out of reach or be ready to cover the dish with your hand if your dog attempts a raid. Gently and slowly, reach out to touch, stroking for a few seconds before feeding a treat from the bowl. The deal you are making with your dog is this: 'if you allow me to touch, I will do so for a few seconds and then feed a tasty treat. If you move or turn away, I will see that you are not comfortable and I will move my hands back immediately, then try again a little later but this time moving more slowly. If you walk away completely, I will wait here until you come back but give up after a minute and try again later with more tasty treats.'

This method gives your dog a huge amount of choice and control over what is done to it and gives it

a way to say, 'no, I've had enough' or 'I don't like that'. The treats help to keep your dog focused on trying to work with you and act as a reward for tolerating a little more each time. Done gradually and systematically by practicing little and often every day, this programme can in time result in a dog that is completely comfortable with any of the body maintenance procedures you need to do.

Try to think of all the things you might need to do to your dog at some point in their lives and get them used to it well in advance by systematically working through the list. This can include anything, from putting imaginary ear drops into an ear to pretending to clip the coat with a beard trimmer with the blades removed. For example:

- **Putting on a collar or harness**
- **Brushing or combing**
- **Drying with a towel**
- **A range of veterinary treatments (bandaging, pretending to put drops in ears or eyes, looking at teeth or opening the mouth, preparing to have blood drawn)**
- **Pretending to put on flea treatment**
- **Nail trimming**
- **Coat clipping**
- **Putting on a muzzle**
- **Putting on a coat**
- **Bathing**

For more information about teaching your dog to be handled sensitively, see the work of Chirag Patel (domesticatedmanners.com), Ken Ramirez (kenramireztraining.com) and the late Dr Sophia Yin, in particular the work of the Fear Free movement (www.fearfree.com).

Helping your dog learn to get used to all of these well ahead of actually having to do them for real will mean that your dog will be both familiar with them and more relaxed about having them done. Since you are both used to doing them, fears or concerns are reduced and you can get them done without stress for both parties.

The more you work on these actions in a positive and friendly manner, offering your dog a choice about whether to be involved or not, but stacking the odds in favour of participation with tasty treats, the more comfortable your dog will become with being handled. Husbandry procedures will become easier and less stressful for both of you. In addition, it will become normal for you to 'ask' and wait for your dog to be ready to accept the action, rather than just

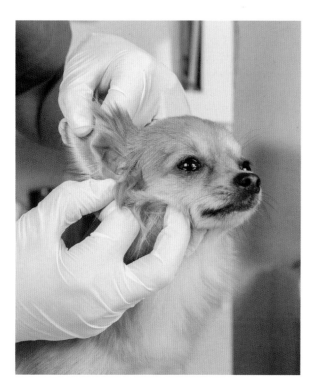

steaming in and forcing your dog to face what you want to do to them, so the trust between you and your dog will grow. Another advantage is that your dog will be able to tolerate necessary procedures that they perceive as being quite stressful or uncomfortable for longer because they have more predictability and a greater degree of control[2].

If a procedure is either a slightly uncomfortable one, such as combing fine hair which tangles and mats easily, or a bit scary, such as wearing a muzzle for the first time, an element of choice for the dog can make the difference between a lifelong hatred of the procedure or being a willing participant. Giving your dog the option to say 'that's as much as I can tolerate today, thank you' when the grooming gets too much to bear or the unfamiliarity of having your face enclosed raises too much anxiety, enables your dog to walk away before their threshold is reached. This is so much less stressful for both of you and allows for future sessions to be tolerated and even enjoyed.

Giving your dog a choice takes some thought and some getting used to if you have always used coercion, however gentle, to get compliance. Once your dog understands it is being given a choice, it will relax much more quickly with each new procedure that you attempt and trust will steadily grow between you. Your sensitivity to what your dog can and cannot tolerate will develop, helping you to be more thoughtful and careful in your actions. Once this becomes common practice, the procedures necessary for caring for your dog's body will become happy experiences for you both, rather than stressful detrimental events that have to be endured. Body maintenance procedures can then become part of your dog's daily mental enrichment (see page 126) and will provide both of you with the fulfillment that comes from a happy sense of cooperation.

Restraint and no-choice handling

Your dog will be very lucky to go through life without any type of restraint or handling where they are given no choice. Busy veterinary staff, groomers, kennel owners, dog wardens or even dog walkers need to get a job done in a reasonable amount of time and cannot always afford to wait for your dog to make choices. This doesn't mean they will be insensitive or lacking in empathy when they do this, but they are usually very experienced at knowing how to efficiently handle animals and your dog may find itself doing what it would not have chosen very rapidly.

For this reason, it is best to help your dog get used to restraint and no-choice handling at home when there are no other pressures or stressors. If you can help familiarize them with what might happen to them at the hands of other people, they can learn that no harm comes to them and they can get used to dealing with the feelings of being out of control and unable to escape in a safe environment with their trusted person before it happens with a stranger. It is best to work on this once you have done all the suggested work on pages 110–13 and you have built up a great deal of trust between you. Trying to do this with no preparation could lead to you causing fear and panic in your dog that would be very difficult for it to recover from.

THE GENTLE HOLD

Begin with a hold that you know your dog can cope with, such as one arm around the chest and the other arm holding your dog's body against you. Gently hold, making sure your dog is standing comfortably without having to use effort to stay upright, for just a few seconds before releasing and rewarding. Different dogs will have different abilities to cope with different actions and you will need to take into consideration what may have happened to them in the past. For example, if a previous owner has dragged them by their collar and punished them, they may be very wary of having their collar held. If this is the case, start with something they can tolerate easily.

Gradually, over many sessions over many days, build up your gentle hold until your dog can tolerate several minutes of being restrained in this way. If, at any time, you feel resistance, hold on until you feel a relaxation in your dog and then release. Having felt that resistance, try to hold for less time next time or hold your dog in a different way so that you can proceed smoothly without causing any concern. (This only applies if you know your dog can cope with the hold. If there are signs of fear or growling, let go and try again later with a less invasive hold or one that is more acceptable to your dog. If you need help, seek the services of a positive and professional behaviourist via referral from your vet.)

Once your dog is totally comfortable with this first manoeuvre, try something else, again gradually

building up the time your dog is held for, but being mindful to go at a speed they can cope with so that they gradually desensitize to it and learn to relax.

In this way, you can slowly build your dog's repertoire of handling procedures that can be tolerated. Try to think of ways in which veterinary staff, groomers, kennel staff or dog wardens (should they find your dog lost on the street) may handle or restrain your dog. If you can build tolerance to at least ten 'procedures' in this way, your dog will be much better placed to cope when no-choice handling and restraint by strangers inevitably happens.

SENSITIVE PROFESSIONALS

To make the most of all this effort you are making to help your dog cope with this type of approach, try

to find professionals who will treat your dog kindly. The sad truth is that some groomers, kennel staff, veterinary personnel or dog walkers have better skills and attitudes to dog handling than others. Finding a set of professionals who are skilled, who care and have your dog's best interests at heart takes time. Be prepared to ask lots of questions and even get referrals from other people who use their service. You will need all your tact and diplomacy to disengage with those professionals you discover to be not so good without causing a fuss, but it will be worth it for your dog to get the best care, particularly if you have a sensitive dog that gets worried easily. Your dog will not have the choice of who to go to, but you do.

Coats and clothes

Many owners of small breeds like to dress their dogs up and may have a range of outfits for different occasions. Some people do not like to see this and feel it is a degradation of their natural beauty, but if the dog is familiarized with this practice slowly and the clothes are put on carefully and with sensitivity, they seem to tolerate them reasonably well. Any clothes that make the dog too hot or are fitted badly so they feel uncomfortable or restricted are a bad idea but, otherwise, there seems to be little harm in it. If, however, wearing clothes means that the dog is carried around all day to keep them clean and they do not get to fulfill their natural behaviour patterns on a regular basis, then clothes are better avoided.

Some dogs have thin fur with little or no fluffy undercoat, or perhaps no fur at all due to a genetic fault or a medical condition. On a cold or wet day, especially if they have to spend a lot of time in a cold environment without exercising, they would really benefit from wearing a well-fitting coat or fleece.

Old dogs who are at the stage of pottering about when outside rather than running may also benefit from a warm, waterproof coat during inclement weather. The extra warmth will help to keep their joints and muscles warm and so keep them mobile. When they get old enough to start falling over on uneven ground, a waterproof coat will keep most of them from getting wet and muddy too. And some dogs with thin natural coats can get cold at night, which can lead them to wake up needing to urinate.

This, in turn, leads to disrupted sleep for owners and so doggy pyjamas or a soft fleece coat can easily solve the problem.

If you would like your dog to wear coats or clothes, introduce them sensitively and use gentle handing at first to give your dog a choice as to how much contact they have with them. This will make putting them on much easier in the long run.

PART 2

THE MENTALLY HAPPY DOG

CHAPTER 1
All you need is love

My client sat down, dropped the lead and started to sob while her dog leapt excitedly around the room investigating new smells and exploring, totally oblivious to the distress of his owner.

Most dogs will respond with concern if their owner is upset and so their lack of relationship was obvious. When she had calmed a little, her reply to my question about how I could help was 'I don't think you can, I just don't like him'.

This sweet fluffy Poodle cross had been adopted only a week ago but was already wreaking havoc at home. He jumped onto tables, jumped up at visitors, chewed things and had nearly swallowed an expensive watch when the owner had chased him and wrestled him to the ground in an attempt to get it back. Gentle questioning of his distressed owner revealed that she had adopted this dog in an effort to replace a dog that had died just two weeks earlier. She and the old dog had lived very happily together for 12 years. 'I loved him so much', she said through further sobs and proceeded to list his excellent qualities and how her new dog compared less favourably.

Different people grieve in different ways and some can successfully get another pet almost at once, while for others it takes time until they are ready to risk loving again. This owner wasn't ready and so could not risk love and friendship with another dog at this time. Most dogs need and crave social connections. For this dog, any reaction, even being told off or

shouted at, was better than being ignored and by rewarding his efforts with annoyance, his owner had successfully taught him to bark, jump and chew to get some of the attention he needed.

Gradually, as she talked, this owner realized that she hadn't been ready and she handed him back to the rescue centre where he found a loving home. He settled in the new home at once, secure in the love that the new owners were able to give him and content to lap up the attention without the need to behave in unacceptable ways. His previous owner took a further six months to collect herself and grieve for her dear departed dog and then she was ready to adopt another.

It may seem unnecessary to discuss love, affection and friendship when most dogs, these days, are companions rather than workers, yet it is a subject so important to the welfare of dogs and so easy to get wrong, that it deserves full consideration. Being a loved member of a social group is as important to dogs as it is to us. It is extremely necessary for a dog's sense of wellbeing and incredibly important for living an optimal life. Without it, or with only partial and insufficient social contact, they will feel as adrift as a human child might in a family where they are unloved.

Emotional creatures

Dogs may have a brain that is not quite as complex as ours or as good at thinking things through, but they are very emotional. They have similar regions and connections in their brains for feeling and registering emotions as we do. They produce the same hormones and chemical changes in their brains that humans do during similar emotional states (for more on this, see the work of neuroscientist Jaak Panksepp on the neural mechanisms of emotion), and, in addition, show similar responses, albeit in their own canine fashion, when they are scared, happy, sad, angry, disgusted or surprised. Dogs may not be so good at the more complex emotions such as guilt, contempt or shame, but they certainly appear able to experience the same intense basic emotional highs and lows that humans experience. Of course, because dogs do not speak, we cannot know exactly how they feel, but as they appear to show all the basic emotions very strongly, it would be wise to assume that they are experiencing them in a similar way to us.

The difference between dogs and humans, however, is that we are mostly free to do something about our negative emotions and seek a solution or a diversion. As many dogs live completely under the control of humans and we often keep them in restricted environments, it is up to us to make sure we care for them on an emotional level to avoid them suffering. In addition, we often have complete control of how much they socialize and with whom, so they are totally dependent on us to offer the sufficient opportunities for them to receive the love they need every day.

How much love is enough?

One way to measure human happiness is to look at the number, strength and quality of personal social connections and as we currently have no other way to measure a dog's happiness level, this seems a good place to start. Dogs are often totally dependent on their family for their social connection because they do not go out to work and some rarely meet others on a regular basis unless dog-loving friends and extended family visit regularly.

If your dog is mostly dependent on you and your family for its social connections, it is worth thinking about the kind of relationship your dog has with each member of the family and whether the total of their social connections each day is sufficient and positive. All too often in a busy family, especially when there are young children to care for and owners are busy working, a dog can get forgotten. Sometimes you may be tired or not in the best of moods yourself, perhaps you have personal problems and have no extra love to give. Usually dogs can cope with the odd day of not getting attention, but when it goes on for too long they begin to unravel emotionally, just as you or I might do if placed in social isolation for too long.

How much love is sufficient will depend to some extent on your dog. Some dogs enjoy regular and frequent attention, while others are content to be more independent. All dogs, however, will need a sense of social connectedness every day. This requires someone to make the time to show them genuine affection and fondness, and to help them feel loved and included in family life.

If necessary, set a timer several times a day to make a connection with your dog. It may sound crazy to have to map out time to spend with your dog, but it is easy for a whole day to pass without paying close attention to others in your family, let alone your dog. While children will have friends and playmates and partners will have work colleagues and friends, the family dog may have no one other than their family and if everyone is busy, it is easy for days to pass without the dog getting any real social connection.

Consequences of life without connection

If dogs get too little love and affection, they can become sad and depressed just as lonely humans can. Over time, they may become withdrawn and unwilling to engage, even when affection is offered. This can have a detrimental effect on their wellbeing and the resulting stress can eventually take its toll on their physical health.

Calm withdrawal may not get much attention from a busy family but frantic 'acting up' behaviour will, so some dogs resort to this just to get some connection with their families. Active, confident dogs rapidly learn to behave in an unacceptable way because this brings them into the spotlight for a brief time while their owners try to control them. A vicious circle of 'naughty' dog/attentive owner is created and, because being told off is never as rewarding as

being loved, these dogs persist with their unwanted behaviour for longer to get the social connection they crave. Not surprisingly, this often causes owners a huge amount of annoyance and distress, not to mention giving the dog plenty of frustration and disappointment too.

Some dogs are the victims of a selfish love that is all about what the owner wants and has nothing to do with meeting the needs of their pet. Owners who use their dog as an extension of themselves or as a way to gain attention are often guilty of this. These owners are often thinking about what they can get from their dog, rather than being concerned about meeting their dog's needs, and so their dog often goes without the real connection that would allow them to feel happy and fulfilled in themselves.

Another dog in the family

Sometimes, a dog's need for social connection is met by another dog in the family. A puppy that finds itself in a family where there is a friendly older dog will soon have a best friend that speaks the same language and plays the same sort of games. Consequently, it may never need to learn human ways and so builds a stronger relationship with the dog in the family rather than the humans.

If you have two dogs and want to test the strength of their relationship with you compared with how much they value each other, you can try this simple exercise with each dog in turn. After an absence of about five minutes, ask someone to bring one of your dogs towards you with your other dog standing level with you but about ten meters away. Bring the dog being tested down a middle path and then allow the dog to divert off centre to greet either you or your other dog. If your dog chooses to greet you first, it has a stronger bond with you than the other dog, but if it chooses the other dog, their relationship is stronger. If you have a dog you raised from a puppy without another dog in the household, it is more likely to choose you. If, however, your dog was raised from puppyhood with another dog in the family, it may choose the other dog over you.

If your dog prefers other dogs to the humans in the family, there may be control issues as the dog may be taking its cues for how to behave from the other dog rather than you. This is particularly likely in a dog that is raised with another dog in the household. Life with a dog that will not listen or respond to you but, instead, does whatever the other dog does, can be frustrating, especially if you have taken on two puppies and neither will do as you ask.

Another problem arises when one of a pair of dogs dies or they have to be rehomed and are separated. This is common when littermates are raised together, or if a puppy is raised with an older dog and then the older one eventually dies. There is usually an extended period of grieving by the dog left behind – they often go off their food, have no enthusiasm for anything and find it difficult to be left alone. This gradually fades but there is often some disruption until things settle.

Life stages

Different dogs will have differing needs for social connection as they go through their lives, but the most demanding times are during puppyhood and old age. During puppyhood, and particularly in the weeks leading up to puberty, all puppies need a strong parental figure to guide and protect them and to give them that vital sense of social connection. Given this strong bond, puppies will thrive and learn quickly – without it, pups struggle to learn and find it much more difficult to become confident and resilient.

This is something to think about if you work away from home most of the day and are considering taking on a young puppy. You could leave them alone all day with only an occasional visitor to feed them and break

up the long wait and they will survive physically, but it is a very unnatural situation and will cause the puppy much mental distress at a time when it should be learning about the world in a happy and relaxed state. This can have detrimental long-term consequences for both your dog and for you.

Similarly, in old age dogs increasingly need someone to look after them and they can become almost as dependent as they were as puppies. They can worry more if this attention is not forthcoming and seem more settled and live longer if someone has the time to truly love and care for them as their bodies start to become increasingly frail as they age.

During adolescence, a dog's need for you is at its lowest although it is particularly important that they have a secure base to come back to if they have an unpleasant experience when they are out exploring. It is all very well to be independent and brave as a teenager, but you still really need a parental figure to be there for you emotionally if you get into trouble.

Different ways to show you care

Affection from owners comes in different forms. It may be praise for doing the right thing, genuine admiration, or it may be physical affection with gentle stroking. Most dogs enjoy their owners taking time to express their love verbally, either on its own or together with gentle touches to the chest or back. It doesn't matter what you say, it is the loving intonation that is important. Spend time with your dog, notice them as you move about the house, talk gently to them, telling them how much you care about them, spend some time doing what your dog wants to do and find ways to include them in daily activities to let them know they are a valued member of your family.

To show affection, some owners put their hands on their dog and rub or pat, usually in the head area, sometimes along the back and sometimes quite roughly. This is often accompanied by enough squeaky verbalization to get the dog animated and stimulated. Dogs often find this type of interaction exciting but also slightly too much, verging on the unpleasant, and may duck their heads away from the hands or move away after just a short interaction.

Even if you have had your dog for a long time, it's a good idea to find out what it does and doesn't like. Try different ways to show affection, using your eyes, voice and hands. Carefully watch for signs that your dog is either enjoying the experience (tail gently waving, moving closer and snuggling up, eyes open and shining, face smiling) or signs that the experience could be too much (tail tucked, head held down, lip licking, yawning, moving away). Just as with humans, all dogs are different, so it is worth spending a few minutes to find out just how your dog likes to receive affection and learn the best way to show you care.

Staying together

All animals tend to show an attention bias towards negative experiences, which can help to keep them safe[1]. This can, however, be counterproductive in social situations where an owner might, for example, occasionally get cross with their dog just because they are having a bad day themselves. Social scientists have found that couples that stay together have at least five positive interactions to every one negative interaction with each other, whereas unstable partnerships are more likely to have a ratio of less than one positive interaction for every negative one[2].

If we assume that dogs are much the same in their social connections, it makes sense for us to try to make sure that all our interactions with our dog are positive rather than negative or that we have at least five positive interactions to every negative interation. Of course, our dogs are not able to file a complaint or request a new home and sadly many are trapped in their relationship with us, but if we want to make them happy it is important to do our best to be as positive with them as possible, even when we are having a bad day.

CHAPTER 2

Leadership

The dog appeared first, a young Bull Terrier cross, barging through the opened door of my office in a rush to see what was on the other side, closely followed by two bickering school-age children and finally two exasperated parents.

After welcoming them, I urged them to sit down and to place a chair leg through the handle of the lead so the dog was kept in one place and to do their best to ignore her so we could talk. Once fastened she made a lunge for the middle of the room, came to a sudden stop as her harness held her back and then started barking, a high pitched rapid and continuous bark that made you want to cover your ears and certainly stopped us from even thinking of holding a conversation. Meanwhile the children had ignored my invitation to sit down and roamed the room, picking things up and pushing their way past things to get to every corner. They eventually found the white board and proceeded to draw on it until their father shouted at them to stop. They did stop after quite a lot of backchat but returned to their seats with the pen and proceeded to draw on each other with much loud squabbling. The dog, having found out that it was fastened, proceeded to flip over and over, tying itself in knots with the lead and eventually settling down to chew itself free.

When I asked how I could help, the owners, with voices raised over the squeals of the children, shouted that their dog was out of control and had been since she was a puppy. She wouldn't do as she was told, barked and mouthed to get her own way and mostly did whatever she pleased no matter how unpleasant the owners found her behaviour.

What was obvious to anyone, except the owners themselves, was how their parenting style had created a family where neither the dog nor the children had very much self-control or many boundaries. Not only did that limit the places that their dog could be taken but no one seemed very happy in the family. The parents were frazzled, the children squabbled and the dog lived in a frantic world of its own making with very little reference to the humans in the family. This family was not calm and harmonious – it was agitated and discordant.

Life for a social animal where there are few rules and no consequences can be just as unsettling as a strict autocratic approach where an owner forces a dog to comply. If you want an optimal life for your dog where its welfare and wellbeing are maximized, you need to find a middle ground where there is order rather than chaos, calm guidance instead of angry shouting, and a feeling that humans are tolerant but in control.

Leadership or domination?

In the world of dogs, the old ideas of dominance and forcing a dog to be obedient are quite rightly outdated. Similarly, punishing and smacking children is now frowned upon and even legislated against. Yet there is no universally recognized way of instilling acceptable behaviour in a family dog (or children for that matter), and there is much debate over whether it can be achieved entirely with rewards or whether some reprimands are also necessary. Parenting skills are usually handed down through generations. Consequently, whether your children or dogs are well behaved or not is likely to depend on what you learned about parenting from your own parents, unless of course you made a conscious effort to learn to do things differently.

In social animals, a leader of some kind usually emerges from the group. In some species, such as chimpanzees, these leaders are despotic and may use punishment to get their way while in others species, such as elephants, leaders are more benign and there is a lot of tolerance most of the time. It is likely that different leadership styles have been shaped by the resource-gathering strategies of the species. Natural hierarchies among dogs have not been widely studied due in part to the fact that most dogs live with humans rather than in the wild, but a recent small study indicated that dogs living without humans form a tolerant hierarchy when living together[1].

Despite a lack of evidence, there is unfortunately a common misconception that dogs need to be dominated and 'kept in their place'. This has arisen partly from the desire to control a spirited predator that lives in our homes and partly from studies made by capturing wild unrelated wolves and seeing what happened when they were put into an enclosure together. Displaced from their family unit, these poor wolves fought frequently and, sadly for dogs, this led to mistaken ideas about dominance and the idea that it is important for a dog to be made to be subordinate. Not only are dogs not descended from wolves (both evolved from a common ancestor thousands of years ago), these captured unhappy wolves were not representative of wild wolves either.

Later studies of free-living wolves showed they live peacefully in family groups, with parents guiding the rest of the pack so they can all be successful in pup care, defense and finding food, with other pack members naturally deferential to their parents rather than being forced to submit.

Life in a social world

To become a valued member of human society, it is important to learn to live within the confines of social norms and to avoid getting into trouble with the law for breaking society's rules. For example, drivers may not like the restriction of speed limits, imposed with the objective of keeping everyone safe, but they know that they have to abide by these laws or they will have to face the consequences.

In a similar way, dogs need to learn the rules of the household. It isn't acceptable, for example, to leap from the floor onto the dining table during Sunday lunch and to start gobbling down the meat from the plates before anyone has got over their surprise enough to stop you (as in the case of a Lurcher I was once asked for help with). In our human world, we expect a dog to behave in certain ways and landing in the middle of the table during lunch isn't usually one of them we find acceptable.

Owners of a newly rescued dog or a puppy need to carefully teach these unwritten 'rules' to prevent bad habits forming. A dog that has been taught to behave well is more acceptable in our society and means you will be able to take your dog to more places. For example, a dog that has learned to quickly settle on cue even when excited can easily be taken to a friend's house without causing a nuisance.

It is better for your relationship if you teach your dog with tolerance, love and attention, just as many good parents might teach their children how to behave. When people lack an understanding of how to teach effectively (rewarding and encouraging what is wanted while ignoring or preventing what is not), they may resort to punitive methods when the dog behaves inappropriately, often justifying this with statements like 'the dog needs to know who's boss'.

Dogs are not issued with a list of house rules on arrival and different people in your household may apply different versions of these rules, so punishing a dog for transgressing a boundary they didn't even know existed is a bit harsh. In addition, a punishment may seem perfectly justifiable to you (dog jumps on table; owner punishes dog), but for the dog that didn't know about the 'rule' the owner can appear to have become suddenly and unaccountably violent which can damage the developing relationship and the dog's trust. Imagine if roles were reversed and, suddenly and unpredictably, a new dog in the family became aggressive to you! It is perfectly possible to teach your dog how to behave acceptably without resorting to threats, intimidation and violence once you know how. Follow the guidelines here and on pages 200–1. If you need further help, find a good dog behaviourist or trainer who uses positive methods (see page 198).

Saying 'no'

Once a dog has been taught the 'rules' of the house and has been well rewarded for showing acceptable behaviour, there is great debate over whether there should be sanctions for non-compliance or not. Sanctions could be as mild as social disapproval or more punitive such as scolding, smacking or worse. Some might argue that there should be sanctions in place if boundaries are overstepped but I disagree. My experience with dogs shows that a dog who 'misbehaves' hasn't yet learned what is required of them or that the rewards on offer for behaving acceptably are not enticing enough.

If you teach your dog patiently with kindness and respect, the relationship you form is so strong that your dog will want to live in harmony with you and will work hard to do so. Mild disapproval when your dog tries something unacceptable is then all that you need to stop the unwanted behaviour and you can easily divert your dog's energy to something acceptable instead. See page 200.

Dealing with frustration

Both humans and dogs have to learn that we can't always get our own way and this is easier to learn when we are young than to grow into adulthood having not done so. In a similar way to humans, an adult dog that thinks its needs come above everyone else's in its social group can wreak havoc when brought into a family.

Dogs particularly have to learn that most of what they want they cannot have, or they have to wait a long time to get it. For example, your dog may want to go for a walk, to run free, to play, but whether or not they get to do this is totally under your control. You may be busy with other things and so your dog has to learn to wait until later or even another day.

Many puppies begin to learn that they can't have all their own way and to cope with the feelings that this causes in the litter when their mother decides to stop her puppies suckling on demand. It may be

much later that a puppy encounters this again, for example, when a collar and lead is used to prevent the puppy running off when it goes outside. The loud high-pitched barking a puppy does while in a veterinary waiting room or on the first day of puppy class is usually the result of the frustration caused by not being able to get where it wants to go. It is the equivalent of a toddler screaming for sweets in the supermarket, not wanting to wait until they reach the checkout. Gradually, through experiencing enough of these situations, most toddlers and puppies learn to be patient, to wait for what they want and to accept and deal with the feelings of loss and anger that happen if they can't get what they want immediately. As an owner, it is important to guide your puppy or dog gently through this process. This entails being mentally smart enough to prevent your dog getting what it wants until it has calmed down and it requires mental toughness to withhold treats, toys and so on from the dog. Some indulgent owners find this difficult, lacking the resolve to make this happen, and often end up living with a dog that makes most of the decisions and becomes angry and sometimes aggressive if it doesn't get what it wants immediately.

Living in harmony

Whether you consider it 'leading' or 'teaching', dogs need guidance to live easily in our human society. The more they understand the boundaries of what is and is not acceptable and learn to enjoy the rewards of staying within those boundaries, the more readily they will fit into our families and our lives.

Dogs seem to do best in families where the parents exert a gentle but firm control over both their children and their dog. Order is present instead of chaos, giving more opportunities for settled harmonious living. Under these conditions, dogs can relax and are free to be themselves, certain in the knowledge they are loved and are not at risk of being shouted at or punished for breaking rules they didn't know existed. Life for a dog with fun sensible owners who are neither too autocratic nor too lenient is great, especially when they offer full protection from any outside threats as well as opportunities to play, explore and enjoy life.

YOUR RESPONSIBILITY

Dogs live in a world where they cannot easily fend for themselves. If you make sensible decisions about how they should live and what they should do and don't let them down even when life is difficult, you will earn their respect and trust. You need to keep your dog fully satisfied both physically and emotionally, and recognize the signs if they are in need. You need to provide a stable environment and be consistently loving towards your dog so they receive all the emotional support they need to be happy.

It is your job to keep your dog out of trouble and protected from danger so you have to be vigilant and plan ahead. You should be aware of things that your dog may find threatening and avoid them and respond quickly if your dog shows signs of distress.

Protecting your dog and providing for their wellbeing is particularly essential at the extreme ages of life or when they are unwell, and your dog will quickly know if you can be trusted. If you are able to do this well, your dog will naturally respect your ability to lead and will be happy to work in cooperation with you.

CHAPTER 3

Sleep and rest

The little Yorkshire Terrier cross had only been in her new home for a week but was running away on a regular basis.

She didn't go very far, she just slipped through a small hole in the fence and trotted off to lie on the lawn of the house next door until her owners realized she was missing and ran to retrieve her.

Her new home consisted of two parents and five young boisterous children. Their parents had raised them well and they were polite and friendly but also extrovert and talkative. They clearly adored their new dog and took it in turns to play with her or stroke her. She seemed to enjoy their company and was friends with them all.

With five happy children, this household was lively and noisy. Their excited high-pitched voices, animated chatter and occasional screams made it hard to concentrate and after being there for just half an hour I began to understand why the dog wanted to escape sometimes. This dog had lived with just one elderly owner for many years who sadly died and left her to a rescue home. She was used to a quiet life where not much happened and there was plenty of time for sleep but her new household was much

busier and there was nowhere she could go where she could sleep and rest undisturbed. It was all too easy for the children to coax her out of her rest to play and get involved with another interesting diversion. Until she adjusted to this new life and became less of a novelty for the enthusiastic children, she sometimes just needed a little bit of peace and quiet and the lawn next door was the perfect place.

Sufficient sleep and rest are essential to a dog's sense of wellbeing. Without them, dogs run at a subprime level, just like sleep-deprived humans. Not only does being tired affect how we feel, it can lead to changes that adversely affect how our bodies and brains function. To keep your dog functioning at the highest level and to give it the best chance of a long and happy life, giving sufficient opportunity for adequate sleep and rest is essential.

Why is sleep important?

All higher animals sleep and need enough good-quality sleep to function well. Humans and animals kept awake for long periods of time die very quickly and, although the true function of sleep is still unknown, we know that sleeping is an essential restorative process that is best done uninterrupted[1].

While there is not much research on a lack of sleep in dogs, we know that sleep disruption in humans and rats can make them prone to infections as well as prone to loss of concentration and mood swings[2,3]. If we assume that dogs deprived of sleep are affected similarly to us, we need to watch out for our dogs becoming grumpy, disoriented or having difficulty concentrating or performing usual tasks. Dog behaviourists receive many more calls about dog aggression problems on Monday mornings after long weekends of activity when the owners have been busy at home for two days than at any other time in the week, particularly if the weather is hot and sunny. The majority of incidents involving aggression are likely to happen on Sunday afternoons when dogs will be at their most tired after a long weekend, so it is important to remember to give your dog sufficient opportunities to rest during busy weekends, holidays and any other time when life is exciting and demanding than usual.

IS YOUR DOG DREAMING?

Researchers have shown that the brain waves of sleeping dogs are similar to those of humans[4]. Just like us, dogs start with short wave sleep and then sink further into deep sleep where there is a greater brain activity and rapid eye movement (REM) sleep). During this time, you may see eye- or muscle-twitching, running-type movement or hear little whimpers or woofs. Is your dog dreaming? We don't know for certain, but the brain wave activity is similar to that in humans so it seems likely that they are.

Sleep patterns

The sleep cycle of dogs is different to the human sleep cycle and is characterized by naturally brief and frequent sleep-wake cycles which are shorter and more frequent than ours. Dogs tend to sleep in cycles of 16 minutes asleep and 5 minutes awake, in contrast to the human cycle of 8 hours asleep and 16 hours awake[5]. This means that during the night while you are sleeping, your dog has an average of 23 sleep/wake cycles (3 per hour). One advantage of these short cycles is that they allow dogs to be much more flexible about sleeping, which is useful for those working, for example, as police or drug-detection dogs – they will find it much easier to cope with changes in their shift patterns than their handlers.

Sleep in short-faced dogs

Many dogs (such as Pugs, Lhasa Apsos, Pekingeses and French Bulldogs) have been selectively bred to have a short muzzle, which comes at a cost to their health and welfare. Short-faced (brachycephalic) dogs have a distorted airway and sometimes struggle to breathe. This is particularly true during exercise, when it is hot (warm air is less densem so oxygen is in shorter supply) and when asleep. Snoring, grunting and wheezing are all signs that they are finding it hard to breathe[6].

Sleeping when the bones of the skull are shorter than average but the soft tissues haven't decreased in size (and so fill up the airways when a dog is relaxed) is particularly difficult. You will often find such dogs sleeping with their heads propped up against a cupboard or the side of their bed in an effort to try to straighten out their airways as much as possible but they must feel constantly short of air and like they may suffocate at any moment.

During sleep there may be times when the soft tissues completely close the airways, resulting in sleep apnea. The English Bulldog, for example, offers a good example of sleep-disordered breathing. In one study, due to their abnormal upper airway anatomy, most Bulldogs were having oxygen saturations of less than 90 per cent for prolonged durations due to obstructive apnea during REM sleep[7]. In contrast, the control dogs never desaturated. As a result, Bulldogs are sleepier than most dogs and they fall asleep very quickly. If your dog is brachycephalic and snores, grunts or wheezes a lot, it may be best to get a veterinary check and possibly treatment or surgery to prevent any negative health consequences.

How much sleep is enough?

Estimates of how much dogs sleep vary widely and it is likely that environmental influences play a big part in how much time an individual dog spends asleep. Although there is no definitive research on the subject, most people agree that dogs will sleep, on average, for about 12–14 hours a day, while puppies can sleep for up to 15–18 hours a day. Most dogs will naturally sleep enough for their needs if given sufficient periods of quiet and somewhere safe and comfortable to sleep.

Just like a tired toddler, young dogs and puppies will get overexcited and irritable when they are overtired. A puppy aged 8–10 weeks, for example, will need a short sleep every few hours. Humans enjoying their new puppy may forget just how much and how frequently a puppy's brain needs to shut down into sleep, and may keep excitement levels high for long periods, especially if children are involved. This can encourage the puppy to stay awake too long. Hard play-biting, together with irritability if restrained, are often the first signs that they are long overdue a nap.

Similarly, older dogs tend to sleep a lot more than adult dogs. An elderly dog will gradually sleep more and more, imperceptibly moving towards rare periods of wakefulness in really old age. Some elderly dogs become confused and restless as night falls or may awake suddenly in an agitated state in the middle of the night, which could be the start of the canine counterpart of Alzheimer's disease[8,9]. Speak to your veterinary surgeon if this happens – they may be able to provide solutions and medications to help with this.

A place to sleep and rest

Dogs will learn to sleep anywhere on any surface, but they probably sleep best on something soft and raised and somewhere near to their friends. If their best friend is you, the obvious place for them to want to sleep is on the sofa or your bed. If you don't want to share, you will need to be really clear and consistent about preventing this and have a good alternative ready – somewhere soft and comfortable, large enough to stretch out at full length, preferably elevated and out of draughts and, most important of all, near to you.

Show your dog where it can sleep, prevent any attempts to get on to your resting places with barricades until they form the good habit of sleeping in their bed and give lots of rewards, including praise and approval, when they go to their own bed. You will need to provide different beds in different rooms since a dog with a strong relationship with you will travel around the house as you move from room to room. A big advantage of giving your dog its own beds is that you can cover them with washable blankets or covers. Washing these regularly will help to prevent your house having a 'doggy' smell that some people may find offensive.

Dogs with lots of fur, such as Newfoundlands or Huskies, however, will be too hot to lie in cosy beds and will prefer to stretch out on a cool floor, preferably in a draughty doorway. This is usually quite inconvenient for humans who have to step over them, but these dogs were bred to survive very low temperatures and often struggle to stay cool enough when living in our centrally heated homes.

Your dog's bed should be its sanctuary in the same way that your bed should be a safe and happy place for you to rest and sleep. Try to ensure that everyone in the family understands that a dog in its bed is off limits and that they should not be disturbed. Your dog needs to learn it can go to its bed if it needs to rest, and children need to learn to leave a resting dog alone. This will also help keep them safe from other people's dogs that may be intolerant of being disturbed and may even become aggressive.

A BED FOR THE NIGHT

Where your dog sleeps at night is a matter of personal preference. Old theories of dominance mistakenly had many owners believing that it was wrong to have their dogs in the bedroom but many owners prefer to have their dog with them while they sleep. This can be beneficial for you and your dog, especially if they suddenly need to toilet in the middle of the night, if they become scared or if some kind of veterinary emergency should strike.

Research has shown that we may sleep better if we have our pets in the bedroom with us, which could be due to the companionship and relaxation they offer, together with an increased sense of safety[10]. Although having them in the same room can be comforting, it is probably not a good idea to have them on the bed, as this can lead to disrupted sleep for everyone.

Dogs are much more responsive to sounds and more alert to dangers when asleep than we are[11], so having them with us while we sleep could indeed make us more aware of approaching dangers. Of course, this could have a negative impact if your dog is in the habit of barking at every disturbance, leaving you feeling a tired nervous wreck. If your dog is doing this, you may need to provide more activity and exercise during the day and solve the barking problem during daylight hours.

NAP TIME

Just like us, dogs may stay awake much longer than usual if there is something stimulating and exciting to do. This can lead to them getting overtired, particularly if they are very young or very old. At these vulnerable ages, be aware of how long your dog has been awake and enforce a nap if necessary by putting them in a quiet room with a familiar blanket and a chew to settle them.

For dogs of all ages, pay attention to how tired your dog is getting during times of high excitement when there are lots of people present (holidays, parties, Christmas) and shut them away for some quiet time to prevent them getting overtired and irritable.

CHAPTER 4

Play

The 5-month-old Rottweiler puppy was excited by my arrival and I could see her bouncing happily up and down on the other side of the baby gate that held her back from visitors in the living room.

Before she could calm herself, she was let through to see me and started a mad race around our legs, her tail between her legs, body arched and legs paddling furiously to push herself forward as fast as possible. She ran up and down the hall and half way up the stairs before racing down and back into the sitting room. As she ran past her large male owner, she leapt up, aiming to reach his sleeve, jaws snapping together as he pulled his arm away just in time.

The owner moved down the hall into the living room and stepped up onto the coffee table, standing there marooned on the only island in the room that his puppy hasn't been able to breach to reach that sleeve and drag him down to play. This puppy was growing fast and it wouldn't be long before nowhere was safe.

While the puppy did the wall of death around the room, jumping from sofa to sofa, and gathering momentum in the open areas, I asked if they ever played with toys together, noting that moving sleeves and trouser legs out of the way as the puppy sped past had become a practiced manoeuver. 'Not really', was the reply (with the owner never taking his eyes of the pup). 'We bought her toys when we first had her but she used to run off with them and now they are all chewed up.' This young puppy had lots of intelligence and energy that was not being utilized in the quiet home she shared with her busy working owners. Although it was currently a fun game for her owner to run and jump to evade her and amusing to watch this big man driven to standing on his coffee table by a young puppy, soon this puppy would be full grown and both big and strong. She needed to learn to enjoy playing acceptable alternative games with toys as soon as possible.

Fortunately, it's not too difficult to channel a puppy's energy into games with toys providing that you know why it is necessary and have the knowledge and tools you need to make it fun. As well as being an outlet for all the predatory behaviour that dogs love to practice, play can be a lot of fun, whether alone, with a human or with another dog. By its very nature, play is rewarding and enjoyable and is an essential part of a holistic approach to dog care. It will enhance your dog's wellbeing, reduce stress, give them the opportunity to exercise and ensure they are living life to the full. Providing appropriate occasions for your dog to play is an essential part of giving your dog the best life possible.

Ready to have fun

As with all social animals, dogs can only enjoy themselves and feel relaxed enough to have fun and play in the absence of stressors and worry. An anxious, frightened or worried dog, or one that has not learned to trust its owners, will not have the motivation to initiate play and is unlikely to respond to invitations. It will, instead, be too busy keeping itself safe and staying out of the way.

Just like us, dogs need to have the right conditions, good social connections and time to relax first before they will consider playing. If your dog is from a rescue centre or when you take on a new puppy, it may be a week or two before it feels settled and relaxed enough to start to have fun and show its true personality.

To empathize with this, think of how it feels to be a guest in someone's house and then add in that they don't speak your language and, worse still, they are not even the same species! You would need time to get used to this before you started to feel at home and perhaps start helping yourself to food or doing something to help you relax. Dogs are really no different to us in this respect. Being patient and kind will speed up this process, as will encouraging good behaviour using a positive approach. Conversely, being strict about enforcing rules you have created and being quick to scold or, worse still, punish, will damage a developing relationship and it will take longer before you can create enough trust and relaxation for your dog to want to play.

Dogs that have had positive existences where people and other dogs were nice to them will often be quick to play and ready to have fun as soon as conditions allow. Just like people, dogs that have been raised kindly will have a sunny outlook on the world and will predict that new encounters with others are likely to go well. Most dogs can be encouraged to play and have fun given time, particularly if their owners are playful and fun-loving themselves, since they are most likely to persist in gently encouraging their dog to come out of its shell and interact. Owners with a sad or controlling demeanor may struggle to get their dogs to play, particularly if their dog has got used to not expecting humans to be much fun.

Children are usually more practiced at having fun and will be a natural fit with a dog's perspective that life is to be lived in the moment and that each moment is an opportunity to have a wild time together. Adult humans, with their full lives of work and duties, often forget or say they don't have time to have fun each day, but one of the joys of dog ownership is that a playful dog will entice you into relaxation and play.

Why play together?

Some dogs will play by themselves in the absence of a suitable playmate, chasing leaves, snapping at flies, running after squirrels in the park. However, most satisfying and acceptable games for dogs involve a playmate, whether canine or human, to add variety, interest and social connection. Play for all species seems to improve mood and physical health and is associated with fun and freedom. It is a great way to relax away from the stressors of everyday life and learn more about the friends you are playing with.

During play, you can learn a lot about each other's strengths and weaknesses, as well as personality traits.

You can learn who is physically stronger, who is more tenacious, which of you is more ambitious to win or possess toys, who gets irritable when things are not going their way and how ready the other is to say sorry if something goes wrong. Playing is an ideal way to get to know a new dog or puppy.

Play between dogs

Play is particularly likely between puppies, littermates and dogs that are new to each other. No one really knows why some dogs enjoy playing together so much, although there is evidence for a variety of benefits, including developing good social relationships, social cooperation and good manners, developing a body that is fit and agile, improving coordination and fine tuning motor patterns that might be needed for hunting[1]. Dogs are one of the only species that continue to play vigorously well into adulthood.

Dogs that are allowed to play with others as they are growing up seem more tolerant of the dogs they encounter in later life and have a greater knowledge of how to keep themselves out of trouble during encounters with dogs less than friendly towards them.

Play between dogs usually involves wrestling, chasing and using their jaws to hold and grapple with the other dog. This is done in a friendly way and there are well-defined, but unwritten, canine rules to the game. For example, a dog will invite another dog to play, watch for signals that the invitation has been accepted, play considerately and cooperatively, then carefully observe when the other dog wants to stop. Dogs that are not so well socialized may misread the cues or play too roughly, disrupting the game or stopping it altogether until they relax and learn better how to play by the rules.

The signals for 'let's play' are an open-mouthed play face, a play bow, a paw lift and soft eye contact.

A variety of ploys are brought in to tempt play, such as play pouncing, an exaggerated retreat and standing in front then jumping backwards and turning around or biting at the air.

If play begins, the dogs will engage in role-swapping and turn-taking, and mixed sequences of play behaviour (such as chasing, wrestling, lying and standing). Self-handicapping occurs when dogs of a different shape, size or fitness level want to play together. The stronger, larger or more experienced dog will adapt their play, self-handicapping to make sure the games are as equal as possible. For example, if a large dog is playing with a puppy, it may well lie down to gently wrestle so that the puppy can play without feeling intimidated or overpowered.

Different breeds of dog will have different play styles that reflect the type of work their ancestors were bred to do. For example, Border Collies usually like to run and chase with others whereas Boxers prefer wrestling games. Play between dogs or puppies with very different play styles can falter unless one or both of them learns to tolerate or play the favourite games of the other.

Play usually stops when one player disengages and walks off, but problems can arise if this signal is ignored. This is more likely to happen when puppies play in unnatural settings where play sessions are intense and unmanaged and there is nothing else to do. The use of aggression by a frightened pup that cannot get the other to stop is common and, once

learned, may be used from then onwards to stop unwanted play.

While some play between dogs is beneficial, too much play with other dogs can prevent a puppy learning how to play with humans with toys. Most puppies prefer to play with other dogs because they play the same games and speak the same language and play with humans takes time and effort. But dogs will usually be more successful as pets if they are focused on humans rather than interested only in members of their own species, so puppies should be encouraged to play much more with people. A good rule of thumb is to play three times as much with a puppy as it is allowed to play with other dogs.

If your puppy plays with other dogs for five minutes in a day, you will need to play for at least fifteen minutes with your puppy in short fun sessions throughout the day. Do this and your puppy will learn to grow up to be human-focused and readily willing and able to play with people. (See page 166.)

Play with people

Play between dogs and humans gives an unparalleled opportunity to build strong bonds and friendships. During play, both parties are equal (ideally) and both are in a happy and relaxed state. Being a playmate allows you to form a shared bond over an enjoyable activity that will last long after the play has ended providing, of course, that the play goes well. Attempts to play with a partner that gets aggressive or controlling will be remembered for all the wrong reasons long after the event.

Play also allows you to channel exuberance into acceptable outlets, so, for example, your dog learns to

sniff out and play with a toy rather than chase joggers in the park. It provides a way to engage all the natural instincts that dogs are born with, such as chasing a ball, pouncing on toys that have rolled to a stop or sniffing them out when they have been hidden in a tall patch of grass.

In general, dogs that play with their owners seem happier and more fulfilled and stand more chance of staying with those owners for life since it is more likely they will build and maintain their relationships within the family. It really is a case of those that play together, stay together.

Wrestling or hunting?

Play with people is very different to how dogs play with each other. Although some people do play rough and tumble games with their dogs, we don't have the physical anatomy, strength or knowledge that a dog has to be really successfully at this game. If owners focus on rough and tumble games as the dog's main outlet for fun, they may not teach or respect the proper rules of engagement. This could lead to their dog learning to start a game without proper invitation and acceptance, to bite hard (although just in fun), to bite inappropriate places and perhaps not to understand the signals that the human wants to stop. This can lead to unwanted behaviour and hard bites, especially in active, exuberant dogs that want to play often.

Take, for example, a large terrier who has been taught to wrestle and bite his young male owner whenever he gets excited and wants to play. Later, in the park, an encounter with another dog leaves this dog energized and excited. Looking for an outlet for his exuberance, the dog spots a small child running. The consequences are obvious, but to the dog, it was just a game. To save such unfortunate incidents, teach your dog to channel their energies into games with toys instead.

When dogs play with toys, they are often playing a type of stylized hunting game where the toy is the simulated prey animal and you are providing the animation of that toy to stimulate different parts of the hunting sequence. Most puppies will follow a small fluffy toy that is wriggled across the ground and thrown into a corner. They will usually chase or stalk and

pounce, grab the toy and come trotting back with it. This follows an instinctive hunting pattern common to all dogs inherited from their ancestors. The full hunting sequence is: track and find – eye and watch – stalk and get closer – chase to get closer – grab and bring

to a stop – kill – consume or stash. All games that are played with toys between humans and dogs focus in on different parts or all of this sequence.

Since playing with toys is very different to the natural play that occurs between two dogs, it will take time for a dog to learn what to do and how to enjoy games with humans and toys. At first they may try to play familiar games they learned with their littermates, biting at moving parts of our bodies when they get excited, but gradually with a bit of perseverance and ingenuity from their owners, together with appropriate toys for the occasion, most dogs can learn to play well with people. Keep in mind that it may take a while until the game becomes fun for both of you. Be prepared to persevere and be aware that your dog may play inappropriately at first.

Dogs from the hound group, such as Greyhounds, Salukis and Bloodhounds, are unlikely to become keen toy players unless you make a great effort to teach them to enjoy them. Even then, they are unlikely to have great enthusiasm for toys once they have matured into adulthood compared with dogs from other breeds. They would rather chase and play with live animals and this can lead to control issues on walks.

Chase games

Chase is a very simple and natural game for dogs to play. Most will play some form of chase game but some breeds, such as those bred to herd (such as German Shepherds and Border Collies), have a stronger inherited propensity for this behaviour. Some dogs have such a strong desire to chase that they will always find something to run after, whether it is cars, joggers, people riding bicycles, horses or livestock. It is much better that these dogs learn to chase toys instead from an early age.

Do not confuse the desire to chase for fun with the desire to chase things away if dogs consider them to be a danger. Some dogs become afraid of the whoosh of cars going past, particularly when they are puppies, and try to chase the car away as it moves past them. Whether it's cars, joggers or children running, this behaviour looks very similar to chasing for fun and it is hard for owners to distinguish between them unless the end of the chase results in some sort of aggression from the dog (although it can result in aggression from the human if people are being chased!).

Once dogs learn to chase toys instead, they will enjoy toys that roll (balls), toys that can be thrown fast (balls on a rope), toys that bounce erratically when they land (asymmetric shapes), or toys that hover in the air waiting to be caught (frisbees). If your dog brings the toy back, the game can begin again. If not, or if they drop the toy and you have to walk quite a distance to find it, the game may not be successful from your perspective and will soon end, so it's a good idea to teach your dog to retrieve.

Bringing a toy back to you once your dog has made the effort to chase and catch it is not a natural behaviour, so you need to teach this systematically and carefully with plenty of rewards if you want it to become a good habit. Some dogs may enjoy keeping hold of toys more than others and may be more reluctant to give them up. A Cocker Spaniel, for example, may be more possessive of a toy than a Boxer and they may need a much higher reward for returning the toy to you than other types of dog. If your dog likes to possess toys and carry them around in its mouth, be sure to give them a long time with the toy after a chase before asking for it back as this is part of the reason they do it and you are more likely to get a willing retrieve if you wait for a while.

Once they have learned what to do, dogs will retrieve regularly for three reasons:

- **To get another chase game. Border Collies that race back with the ball and spit it at your feet fall into this category and will play this game over and over for as long as you will keep picking up the toy and throwing it.**
- **To please you. If you are constantly delighted that your dog returns the toy and gives it back, and your dog enjoys your praise and adoration, it will keep returning the toy for as long as adoration is sufficient to outweigh the effort of returning the toy. However, this is usually a fairly weak reward and so is unlikely to last for more than two or three throws. Working dogs kept outside in a kennel often crave social connection and may work for this reason for longer than a pet dog who receives love and affection on demand.**
- **To get a reward for bringing the toy back, such**

as a tasty treat. Again, once the dog has learned this, they will continue to retrieve until the effort involved outweighs the desire to earn the treat offered.

CHASE IN MODERATION

Chase games played well are a useful energy outlet, a safe way to fulfill the desire to chase and a good way to keep your dog fit, but it is very easy to play the chase game to excess and dogs that have a natural propensity for this game may become obsessed with it. Too much chase can cause excessive wear and tear on the body, especially on the foreleg joints that take most of the impact as the dog catches and turns (dogs will usually turn on one favoured leg repeatedly

when playing this game) and this can lead to arthritis and mobility problems in the long term. In addition, repeated manic chase games that are not balanced with other types of behaviour are unnatural and can lead to overarousal, leaving your dog wired and full of adrenalin which may result in hyperactivity in the house and an inability to settle.

Play chase games in moderation and pair them with less active games and training to provide a balance between exercise and mental activity. Sometimes it is difficult for owners to do this because of the ease and vigour with which some dogs play chase but check the time you spend throwing toys for your dog and try to balance it with at least three times as long engaging in other activities that result in calm thinking for your dog. (See page 195.)

Tug of war

Some dogs, often the Bull Terrier breeds, enjoy tug of war play more than any other game. During this game, the tug toy, usually a thick rope or ragger, takes the brunt of the bites, so make sure it is long enough to put a good distance between jaws and fingers. As this is quite a physical game, teach good manners for play from the outset. All dogs are individual and some dogs that like to tug are very strong, so it may be wise to find a good dog trainer who can help you do this. Things to teach include:

- Don't start until I invite you to
- Stop when I ask
- Stay at your end of the toy and don't try to grab the end near to my fingers
- Be careful around my fingers and stop playing immediately if you accidently find a human in your mouth instead of the toy

Once dogs learn these rules, they usually play kindly and fairly, biting only on the toy and never extending the game to clothing or limbs. As this game is very physical and teeth will be close to skin, it makes sense to keep tug of war games short and always stop before your dog gets too excited. Too much arousal and excitement can lead a dog to the point where it is not thinking carefully, so be vigilant and end the game while the dog is still relatively calm.

Pounce and shake

Some dogs, particularly terriers, enjoy capturing and chomping on small toys that squeak. They may pounce on the toy once it has rolled to a stop, grabbing it in their mouths and biting to make it squeak loudly and repeatedly. They may shake it vigorously from side to side and if left alone with the toy proceed to hold it firmly between their front feet in order to dissect it to get to the squeaker inside.

This type of game can be quite solitary – use two squeaky toys and allow your dog to play with them one at a time so you always have a squeaky toy as a reason for your dog to come back to you and so stay involved in the game with you.

Hide and seek

You can play hide and seek games with objects, toys, food and even people. These games can be as simple as hiding your dog's favourite toy under a cushion and encouraging a search of the sofa until your dog sniffs it out, or you could get each family member to hide in the garden and help your dog track them down.

Once dogs have learned what to do, the act of sniffing things out is very easy for them. It can seem quite amazing that a dog can find objects or people by scent alone and owners will often make a big excited fuss of their dog when they make a find, making the whole game incredibly rewarding for the dog.

Try extending this game by gradually increasing complexity and difficulty. For example, you could start with a search for a toy that is just out of sight in one small area and gradually extend the difficulty until your dog is searching the whole room or even the whole house for a toy that is buried at the bottom of the toy box. All dogs that detect bombs, drugs and even people lost on a mountainside or buried in rubble are trained in a similar way.

Hide and seek games rely on a dog's incredible ability to detect minute traces of scent, which is roughly ten thousand to one hundred thousand times more sensitive than ours[2,3]. Humans have about five million receptor cells for scent in their noses, dogs have about two to three hundred million. Put another way, the surface area of the cells in our nose that detect smells is roughly 5cm² compared with 150–170cm² for dogs[4] and the area of their brains dedicated to scent is much larger than ours, allowing them to process all that extra information easily. Where we might notice a spritz of perfume in an enclosed room, a dog would have no trouble smelling it in an enclosed stadium[5]. These types of games use up a lot of mental energy because the dog is processing information and has to make decisions based on what it finds along the way. This, together with the physical workout involved in running everywhere to find the scent plumes and trails, results in a tired fulfilled dog that has used its natural abilities to the full. It's an extra bonus if they entertain us or are useful in the process.

Tips for successful games

- Playing with your dog should be fun. It is not work or training, so try to relax and enjoy it – it will be most fulfilling for your dog if you play in a lighthearted, child-like and joyful way. Play needs social connection, cooperation, equality and fairness for the game to continue and to be satisfying, so if both players are enjoying the experience, it will last longer and is likely to happen more often.
- All dogs, just like their owners, are individuals. What one dog likes may not be fun for another, so try to find the game your dog likes to play the most.
- Be fully present in the process when you play with your dog. Playing is about social connection as well as physical activity and if you're looking at your phone or doing something else while you play, the experience will be much less fulfilling for your dog.
- Try not to be too controlling or possessive of the toy and if you are really not in the mood, play for a very short time only. Walk away if you start to feel annoyed or frustrated rather than poison later games by being cross enough to give your dog a bad experience.
- Be inventive and learn new ways to play to keep things interesting for you both. Keep games short and sweet and try to play often throughout the day. If you have a busy life, remember to find time to play or set electronic reminders so you don't forget.
- Keep favourite or fragile toys out of reach of your dog but in places where they are easily accessible to you.

- Take some toys out on walks and leave other toys down for your dog to play with on their own when they wish.
- Use a soft fluffy toy for a puppy or a new dog, keep it wriggling close to the ground and dart it in and out of view. Occasionally throw the toy fast along the floor racing it past your dog to encourage a chase. Leave the toy with them for a while to let them experience the joy of possession, rather than trying to get it back again immediately.
- Try putting food inside a toy for older dogs that have not yet learned to play to help develop their interest in toys. Help them to discover the food inside at first and they will soon become interested in playing with these toys. You can buy toys that open up and close around food.
- When you have built up interest in toy play, teach clear rules for some games to help you have more control. Games usually build lots of excitement in a dog and if you can gain control during times of excitement, control at other times will be easy. For example, teach an emergency stop while chasing or an immediate drop when tugging. You may need to find a dog trainer to help you learn how to do this.

CHAPTER 5

Living without fear

The small puppy sat looking around at the rest of the class, ears pressed tightly back against his head, tail tucked underneath, head swivelling in all directions as he responded to every sound.

A young child ran past, moving close to him to get to her family and the puppy retreated, squeezing himself into a small ball under his owner's chair, his huge eyes peering out from a body that had started to shake.

So many puppies start life with a similar lack of confidence and often grow into adults that have fears and anxieties in later life. These emotions are generated in similar parts of a dog's brain to ours and result in similar neurons and hormones being activated[1]. Understanding this and given that dogs will avoid frightening situations whenever possible, it is hard not to conclude that they feel exactly as humans do when afraid.

Most owners are very protective of their dogs and will try their best to keep them safe. Mental stress, however, is underestimated and needs to be considered carefully when choosing how your dog lives and what may be worrying or frightening on a daily basis. For optimal living, you need to take steps to help them learn to cope. The absence of mental stress is necessary for a long and happy life and living as stress-free as possible should be a goal for us all.

Most fears originate from a lack of experience when very young. Puppies that grow up in a household where they're exposed to a wide variety of situations in their first 3–16 weeks will take most things in their stride later in life but pups kept in barren environments (such as a barn, a kennel or a puppy farm cage) will be much more afraid of anything new at a later date[2]. Some fears, however, arise from unpleasant experiences and this is why it is so important to ensure that a new puppy has someone to protect them while they learn and to use positive methods to teach them how to fit into human society.

When a human or dog thinks it is under threat, this leads to anxiety even if there is no actual threat present. Anxious dogs will be hyper-vigilant, looking and listening intently to what is going on around them in order to detect a threat. Some stressors will be obvious, such as if a dog is afraid of strangers, and some will be more obscure, the whooshing a boiler makes as it turns on, for example. You may need to carry out some clever detective work to figure out what it is that is frightening your dog.

Finding out how your dog responds to threats and the body language shown when scared or under pressure is important if you are to optimize your dog's wellbeing with a stress-free existence.

Responding to a threat

For any animal faced with a sudden threat, there are four basic options: run, fight, freeze or appease. Which one your dog chooses will depend on factors such as the nature of the threat, speed of approach, your dog's confidence levels and its previous experiences. The response you need to avoid is the 'fight' option.

Once a dog or puppy learns how effective being aggressive can be (usually the threat pulls back and the owner pulls the dog away), aggression becomes more likely the next time the dog encounters this situation and it forms a dangerous habit. To stop this happening, always be vigilant and watch for signs that your dog is not happy. It is important to step in to protect your dog – move your dog away from whatever is scaring it. Do this and your dog will not learn to be aggressive and will instead learn to trust your good judgment and rely on you when events take a scary turn.

All the photographs in this chapter show dogs that are somewhere on the range of 'not comfortable' to 'very scared'. Compare these with photographs elsewhere in the book and you will see the differences. Watch your own dog and find out what signs they show when they are not happy so that you can act to help them faster. Signs to watch out for are:

- **Ears pulled back**
- **Whites of eyes showing**
- **Tense face and body**
- **Tail lowered or between the legs**
- **Tail and body stiff, even if tail is wagging**
- **Raised front paw**
- **Yawning**
- **Fast panting even on a cool day**
- **Lip-licking**
- **Shaking**
- **Sweaty paw marks on the floor**
- **Sudden shedding of coat**
- **Looking away/moving away**
- **Trying to hide**

Long-term consequences

Most animals, even fish, have a sophisticated fear response designed to keep them safe from threats and this is very useful in a dangerous world. If a rhino is charging towards you at full speed, your sympathetic nervous system will quickly shut down all non-essential bodily processes, such as digestion, and accelerate any that you need to get you out of trouble, such as increasing your heart rate, breathing rate, blood flow to your muscles, and even expanding your pupil size so you can take in more of the essential information about the threat. Once the danger has passed, your parasympathetic nervous system takes over and returns everything to normal. This process is the same for dogs as it is in humans[3].

Problems arise when threats are not one-off events but are long-term anxieties and fears, such as where a dog is either ill-equipped for life as a pet, or it is subjected to stressful events on a daily basis. For example, they may be scared of another dog in the household, or a toddler in the family or one member of the family may be particularly unkind. Situations like this keep a foot on the fear accelerator and the sympathetic nervous system is activated for long periods of time.

As well as being very unpleasant for your dog, long-term stress can have serious consequences for their physical health, particularly weakening their immune system resulting in more visits to the vet. Long-term stress has also been shown to contribute to or aggravate gastrointestinal diseases, dermatologic conditions, respiratory and cardiac conditions, behavioural disorders and to shorten a dog's lifespan[3].

Since it is impossible for dogs to solve these issues, it is up to us as guardians responsible for their wellbeing to recognize when they might be worried or scared and to help them out. Their limited ability to think and their lack of freedom to regulate their environment (which we often have complete control over), leaves them vulnerable. They need our help to ensure they feel safe whenever possible.

A sense of safety

It is essential to find out what makes your dog anxious or afraid and then avoid stressors or help your dog to learn to cope with permanent horrors if your dog is to be stress-free.

Many owners do not see or recognize the signs that their dog is worried but if you watch them closely and know what to look for (see page 180), you will be able to tell when your dog is feeling uncomfortable. It is usually easy to know when dogs are very afraid (although these signals may be masked in some dogs with lots of thick, curly dark fur or in breeds developed not to show signs of distress, such as Rottweilers or Japanese Akitas) but it is often harder to spot more subtle signs of discomfort and unease.

Dogs can be afraid of many things that will not actually harm them. It does not really matter if they will be harmed or not, they think they will be and so it is wise to treat the threat as a real one. For example, a dog may be very afraid of a toddler if it has not met any in its formative months because toddlers look and behave very differently to adult humans. The dog's owner may know that the toddler is not a threat to the dog, but the dog will not be convinced by its owner's attempts to draw them closer.

Show some understanding that your dog is afraid, both at home and when outside, and help your dog to move away or move the stressor away to allow your dog to feel supported by you and give it time to calm down. This can be challenging if the stressor is another human or another dog because you may feel you have to be polite and sociable rather than to put your dog first. Say you have a shy young puppy that sees a person approaching and tries to get away but is prevented by its lead. In that situation, the best approach from the dog's point of view is for the owner to turn around and walk away which will immediately reduce the puppy's fear and prepare the way for solving the problem slowly later. However, unless you spot the early signs and turn away in advance, it can be awkward to turn away when the person approaching has spotted your puppy and wants to say hello. Always be on your dog's side when it comes to fears and learn to avoid frightening situations – this will give your dog a lot of confidence in your ability to handle situations and will help them relax and feel safe under your protection.

Sometimes there will be stressors in your dog's life that you can't avoid – if you move to a house where

your dog is very disturbed by noises that it can hear through the walls, for example, or if a new partner moves in and your dog finds itself living with a cat it is scared of. In these circumstances, you need to help your dog to learn that the stressor is harmless using a programme of very gradual safe exposure as well as by pairing the stressor with pleasant events, such as games or treats. If your dog is very scared, though, I recommend you seek professional help from a recommended animal behaviourist.

If you cannot avoid certain stressors, scientific psychological studies suggest that you need to maximize your dog's control of the scary situation, maximize predictability of when and how a stressor

will occur and maximize opportunities for your dog to do something to help it cope with the resulting fear or frustration[3].

It's also important to take a good look at your own stress levels and think about how they may be affecting your dog. Our pet dogs are usually very attuned to how we are feeling and can tell by our actions and by the way we smell if we are upset. If you are experiencing stress on a prolonged and regular basis, your dog, as well as yourself, will also be adversely affected by this chronic stress[4]. Take a long look at the stresses in yourself and your family and try to find a way to tackle them, for your own sake and for the sake of your dog!

Stress when left alone

Some estimates have put the number of dogs that are anxious when left alone as high as 50 per cent and your dog is more at risk if it has had no specific isolation training or if it has had more than one home. If you are able to leave a camera set up to monitor what your dog does when it's left on its own, you will be able to see for yourself if it is stressed or not.

A relaxed dog may eat any food left down and will soon settle into a deep sleep. If your dog ignores food, paces for some time, barks or is destructive or settles restlessly, always keeping alert for possible intruders, it is likely that they may be anxious all the time you are not there. Long-term anxiety caused by being left for long periods of time on a regular basis could be harmful and it is worth consulting a good professional specializing in behavioural change to see if you can help your dog to feel more comfortable about time it has to spend alone.

THE 5:1 RATIO

All animals (humans included) tend to focus on and remember negative experiences more than the good ones as it helps them to stay safe. It is sensible to pay more attention to things that might hurt or kill you, but it means that they can sometimes focus too much on the memory of bad experiences even if there was no real danger[5].

Researchers have found the ratio of five good experiences to one bad experience helps to overcome fear, so if a bad thing happens to your dog, you may need to help them get over it by arranging for at least five good experiences in a similar situation[6,7].

CHAPTER 6

Exercising the mind

When we got to the bottom of the hill, I realized I'd left my tracking harness in the middle of the field.

Looking back at the enormous field, I realized my chances of finding it were poor, especially as it was made of grass-coloured webbing.

My rescue dog, Beau, and I were learning how to track and I had been so pleased when he'd found the article put out by the tracklayer that I'd sat down to congratulate him, taken off his harness and rolled up the tracking line. I'd been preoccupied (there's a lot to think about when you first start tracking) and I'd left the harness on the ground and walked off. Fortunately, my teacher and friend Tony Orchard had his experienced working trials dog Loki, a German Shepherd, with him. When I explained my error, he took Loki, walked up the field a short distance and then, indicating the place at the top of the hill where we had been working, he gave his dog the signal for searching and set him free.

Loki set off like he knew what he was doing, nose up scenting the air. He ran almost straight to where we had been working, weaving a little as he sniffed the area for scent. He began to quarter the ground, zigzagging back and forth over the area, then he dropped his head to the ground and began to move more slowly. Within seconds, he'd found it, grabbed it in his jaws and raced back down the hill before presenting to his owner. Tony took it quietly and spent some minutes gently praising his dog and letting him know how amazing he was. Loki, sides heaving and tail gently waving, looked like he had enjoyed the very successful effort he had made for the much-loved human in his life.

At the time this happened, I was at the beginning of my career with dogs and it made a huge impression on me. Not only had I seen a dog do something effortlessly in minutes that would have taken a human hours of searching, but I was impressed at how willing this dog was to make such an effort for his owner and how well trained he was to know what his owner was asking for. The love and cooperation between them were truly beautiful to witness and it's something that I have tried to emulate ever since.

When you hit that sweet spot of working with a willing dog to achieve something that neither of you could do alone, there is nothing else quite as fulfilling and it seems to be very rewarding for the dog to use its natural talents to do something it's been trained to do well. Having enough to do and doing things that provide fulfillment is essential to a dog's wellbeing. Mental activity is even better if the process of thinking and learning can be combined with happy social interaction and providing this type of experience on a daily basis can really enhance their satisfaction with life.

Mental exercise and contentment

Dogs enjoy solving problems, just as we do; the only real difference is that the problems need to be simpler. Historically, dogs either worked for their living or were free to wander and do what they chose, so they had plenty of mental stimulation and activity. Many pet dogs in the modern world live lives that are much more restricted. They live within the confines of houses or back gardens and usually don't go out unless accompanied by their owner. Consequently, they can become bored and frustrated unless their owners provide sufficient mental stimulation or include their dog in all aspects of their busy lifestyle.

Sadly, and completely contradictory to their natures, it has become common practice to keep dogs in a small crate for part or all of the day as if they were a piece of machinery that could be packed away when it wasn't needed. This considerably reduces their opportunities for freedom and the chance to make their own decisions about what they do.

In our modern world, dogs and humans often live at the opposite extremes of the mental exercise scale. Owners are often mentally overstimulated thanks to long working hours and busy lives – they can fill every waking moment with activity using books, TV and radio, mobile phones and other electronic devices. We are so stimulated by life that we often need to use mindfulness or similar prompts to remember to slow down mentally.

Many dogs, on the other hand, are often confined for hours with little to do other than sleep and rest while their owners are at work or doing things that don't include their dog. While this lifestyle can be challenging for many dogs, it can also be a struggle for busy tired owners, particularly if they have children, to find enough time and energy to give their dog the mental stimulation it needs to feel content.

A meeting in the middle is possible if you use contact with your dog as a way to relax. For example, you could include your dog in your exercise regime instead of going to the gym or make a similar substitution so you are actively engaged with your dog for more of the day. Your dog then receives the stimulation and mental engagement it requires to feel fulfilled and the extra contact with your dog gives you a chance to take time out from your busy world. If you understand how important mental stimulation is to your dog and you are prepared to make some changes to your routines and habits, you will both benefit.

Different dogs need different amounts

Each dog is different and will need different amounts of daily mental activity. Some will need a lot whereas others are much more content to sleep and rest for longer periods.

Genes play a part in how mentally active a dog is likely to be. Dogs descended from working dogs are likely to be much livelier than those bred from generations of pet dogs. The herding breeds, for example, generally consist of dogs with a good work ethic and boundless energy, both physical and mental – Border collies and German Shepherds, for example,

really love to work and engage in mental activity. They enjoy thinking things through as well as working with their humans to solve a problem. Bichon Frise and King Charles Spaniels, on the other hand, are much more content to relax for more of the day and not put in the mental work needed to learn complex tasks. Checking out your dog's genetic history and what propensity for mental activity it might have will help you judge how much is enough.

How mentally energetic a dog is will also depend on how it has been raised. Some dogs will have grown

up in very quiet homes and have learned to rest and sleep for much of the day. For these dogs, loud parties and family gatherings that go on too long can make them irritable and very tired. Another dog might have grown up in a household where there was something interesting going on every minute of the day, so long periods of rest and quiet can be difficult for them to cope with.

As the trend for puppy socialization and positive training grows, it is becoming more common for puppies and young dogs to receive plenty of stimulation in the early months with their new owners. Owners make lots of effort to establish good manners, play lots of games with their dog,

and spend time doing homework from training classes to teach their dog the appropriate response to cues and signals. This takes up a lot of time during puppyhood and the puppy learns to be well behaved and responsive.

Gradually, however, there is a tendency for owners to lose focus and assume the job is done now that they have a dog that fits well into the family, but the dog will miss the positive training and play when it stops. They have increased the connections within their brains as a result of all the activity and are now primed for action, so be aware that once you introduce an activity, your dog will expect it to continue – once you have started, do not stop!

The consequences of a quiet life

If a dog has the mental capacity to be thinking for a large proportion of the day but is kept in the quiet confinement of a house without very much to do, there will be consequences. These may not be immediate – dogs can be quite forgiving and can cope with a few days of rest and boredom – but if this situation goes on for too long, you will often begin to notice a restless energy that is likely to explode into unacceptable behaviour whenever there is any excitement. This could take the form of wild barking at the slightest noise and rushing to investigate any potential disturbance. Or the family may be targeted as possible sources of entertainment and your dog may become crazily boisterous and demanding whenever you move. Alternatively, your dog may take out its desire to do something, anything, on items it finds lying about, or taking them from surfaces and counters to chew them to pieces.

All sorts of 'naughty' dog behaviour inside the home can be the result of too little to do. This is particularly likely in young dogs, and especially those who are going through adolescence as this is a time when a young dog would naturally travel further afield exploring the world. Without this freedom and the mental exercise that comes with it, a young dog kept confined can become very bored and may make every effort to relieve that boredom by acting in ways that the owner would rather they do not.

You may prefer your dog to lie down and sleep for most of the time but there is only so much sleeping and resting that a dog can do, even when it is getting plenty of physical exercise each day. Dogs need to be busy and active for at least part of the time when their owners are with them and if they are to be left at home for a long time, they need to have things to do. If they don't, be prepared to cope with the consequences of living with a dog that is a bit too full of mental energy and likely to behave in challenging ways.

It really is easier to provide an outlet for this mental exuberance rather than try to suppress it – dogs have a rather limited ability to think compared with us, so it doesn't take too long to mentally tire them. As with physical exercise, providing sufficient mental activity every day will soon become part of your routine and your reward will be a calm, contented dog that is a joy to have around.

Opportunities for mental activity

There are many ways to provide your dog with mental exercise. The easiest is probably to train your dog to behave well so it can be included in as many aspects of your life as possible and taken to as many places as dogs are allowed to go. If you also make the most of any opportunities that present themselves to give your dog some fun mental exercise, you can build this into your life with your dog rather than having to make an extra effort to set time aside or to find additional places to do this.

All these activities will provide mental stimulation for your dog:

- training and learning
- sniffing and finding exercises
- games and fun (see pages 168–76)
- working walks (see pages 26–31)
- playing with other dogs
- puzzles and tricks
- outings and exploration
- sports that you and your dog can train for and take part in, such as agility training, doggy dancing, Canicross or working trials

It may be a good idea to try a little bit of everything and see what you and your dog most enjoy. All of these activities will require some time and effort to learn initially but the benefits for both of you will make this extra work worth it as your dog will have more fun, giving you a happier and easier life.

Training and learning

All training and learning will exercise your dog's brain with the added bonus that you can teach your dog cues and responses that will make life with your dog easier. For example, if you want to take your dog to a dog-friendly café or pub, or to visit your friend, it is really helpful if your dog knows:

- How to come back when called so you can go for a good working walk first to get rid of excess energy.
- How to stay calm while you clean their fur with a towel so you do not arrive with a muddy dog that will leave dirt everywhere.
- How to walk nicely on a loose lead to enable you to walk in and create a good first impression.
- How to lie down and rest or sleep on a mat at your feet until you are ready to go.

Contrast this with a dog that arrives full of energy, lunging this way and that on its lead, jumping up at tables or at people and then can't keep still or quiet while you try to relax and talk to your friends.

All of this requires good teaching at home and then in as many places as possible, without distractions and other temptations at first, and later with disturbances going on around you, both with your dog in a calm state and then when full of excited energy. If your dog can learn the cues for how to behave well and then learns to respond to those cues in whatever circumstances you find yourselves, you will have a dog you can take anywhere. Of course, this all takes time and effort, as well as a good relationship and cooperation, but it is good mental activity while your dog is learning and eventually you will have a dog you can easily take out and about to get more of that mental activity in a more natural setting.

Finding a good dog trainer to help you with training will be invaluable. Not only will they teach you what to do to train your dog, they will support you and keep you on track to achieve your goals. There are plenty of good books about dog training and other sources of information but a good trainer will make it much easier. Whether you join a class or hire a trainer to help you privately, it is essential to find a knowledgeable teacher who you and your dog get on with. Ask friends or other dog owners for recommendations and be prepared to try out two or three until you find one who is right for you.

It is essential that your dog trainer uses only positive methods. In the past, coercion and force were used to train dogs and, unfortunately, there are plenty

of trainers around who are still doing this. Positive methods that use rewards and fun to teach your dog how to respond willingly are much kinder and will help you build a strong relationship with your dog based on trust, as well as building a solid foundation of understanding for your dog that can be built on over time. Outdated punitive methods will erode your dog's confidence and cause mistrust and fear that will eat away at the bond between you. If your trainer uses mostly positive methods for training but wants to punish unwanted behaviour, walk away. Trainers with limited knowledge tend to fall back on punishment when they get out of their depth, so find someone who knows their subject well. Positive trainers will help you train your dog faster and help you develop a much better understanding of training, which will eventually mean you can continue unaided.

Once you know the training principles and what is needed to help your dog learn cues for a certain action, it is relatively easy to use these principles to train for almost any situation. You will need to learn:

- **How to prompt different actions that you want to reward.**
- **How to fade the prompt and introduce a cue.**
- **How and when to reward and why it is necessary to teach each exercise in different contexts.**

When selecting a trainer, make sure they know how to develop your training to help you teach the cues during distractions and at a distance, how to build duration and how to keep attention focused during periods of excitement.

KEY TRAINING TIPS

Be positive rather than negative. All animals tend to focus on and remember negative experiences more than good ones. This helps them stay safe by paying attention to things that may damage them. However, it can also mean that they focus more on what you might be cross about than when you show approval[1]. If you cannot stop yourself from showing disapproval towards your dog during training, research has shown that for every one disapproval, you need to give five approvals for learning to be effective. Ideally, you should train your dog without showing disapproval but at least aim for a ratio of five positives to every one negative[2,3] (also see page 187).

Make lessons short and fun. Have a sunny outlook to training so that you gently encourage your dog to behave in a way you prefer. Remember what lessons were like for you at school – the most inspiring teachers probably made lessons fun and interesting by breaking them into easy chunks. Do the same for your dog to stop them getting bored and frustrated.

Keep lessons simple and straightforward. Remember, the part of a dog's brain that processes thinking is much smaller than in humans. If your dog is not learning what you are trying to teach, change the method, make it easier or try again later once you have worked out what is going wrong. A good dog trainer can help you when things are not working

out and you should never feel like dog training is something you should know how to do naturally. A good professional will take years to learn the skills and knowledge needed to train animals effectively so never be afraid to ask for help.

Once you have learned the principles for training your dog how to respond to cues, you can encourage your dog to have good manners

and to behave well in all settings. The more you can reward and encourage good behaviour, the more often your dog will behave in an acceptable way and any unacceptable behaviour patterns will tend to disappear.

A good dog trainer or professional who specializes in behaviour problems can help you deal with stubborn or persistent problems (ask your veterinary surgery staff for a referral or recommendation).

Plan your training. Before you begin the process of training, list the requirements you have for your dog with those most important for your lifestyle first. What cues does your dog need to respond to in order to live easily within your household? Everyone's requirements will be slightly different. You may have someone in the family who likes to walk your dog but is a little infirm, so it is essential that your dog does not pull on the lead. Or your dog may have a long coat that needs regular attention, so it is important for them to learn to stand up or lie down or keep still on cue so they can be groomed easily. Teaching cues that you will use routinely and are important to you will help keep you focused and give you the incentive to keep going.

TRAINING REWARDS

No discussion on training is complete without mentioning the rewards used to encourage your dog to do what you ask. Rewards for your dog mostly take the form of meaty treats (see page 80) or games with toys.

Rewards are like wages – it is unlikely that most people would continue to go to work unless they received regular wages. If you ask your dog to make an effort for you or to stop doing something they would rather do instead, most will require regular payment to keep them working and keep responses sharp. You may be lucky enough to have a dog with a strong work ethic that will make an effort just to please you, but most pet dogs receive love and attention for doing nothing at all and so are unlikely to work hard for it.

To help with your training, it is useful to know which rewards your dog prefers. While one dog may prefer a tug game, another may prefer a chase. Some will sell their soul for a small piece of warm sausage, others may prefer dried liver. Work out your dog's hierarchy of rewards by giving choice tests in different situations and rank all rewards you can use in training from high to low to help you decide which rewards to use for which task (although be prepared for this to change frequently). Tasks that require a lot of effort, such as coming back when called when they were playing with other dogs in the park, will need your highest value reward. Tasks that are easy once learned, such as sitting next to you at the kerb while you are waiting to cross the road, can be rewarded by something from lower down the list.

In conclusion, positive training brings a wealth of benefits to your dog. Not only can the process of learning be mentally enriching in itself but it can also result in great responses to cues and the development of acceptable behaviour that enable you to take your dog out and about. This will provide even more mental exercise and activity.

TRAINING EXAMPLE – BEING WEIGHED

I have seen plenty of dogs, some quite unwell, dragged onto scales against their will and pushed and pulled to keep them in position while the machine reads an accurate weight. This is never pretty to watch and must be stressful for the dog at a time when they are not feeling their best. It is so much better to be able to give your dog a cue to move forward to the scale, a cue to stand still once in position, and then to reward well once the weighing is done. See page 113 for sensitive handling exercises.

You'll need a small platform of a similar size and height to vet's weighing scales so you can practice at home. Train your dog to walk voluntarily onto the platform, teaching a cue for this as well as one for keeping still. Some further training with the platform alongside a wall, as it often is in the vets, is needed, together with training in different places, with distractions, and then, finally, some real life training using the weigh scale at the vets. If all this is done in advance with a dog that is well, getting an accurate weight when your dog is unwell is going to be easy and stress free.

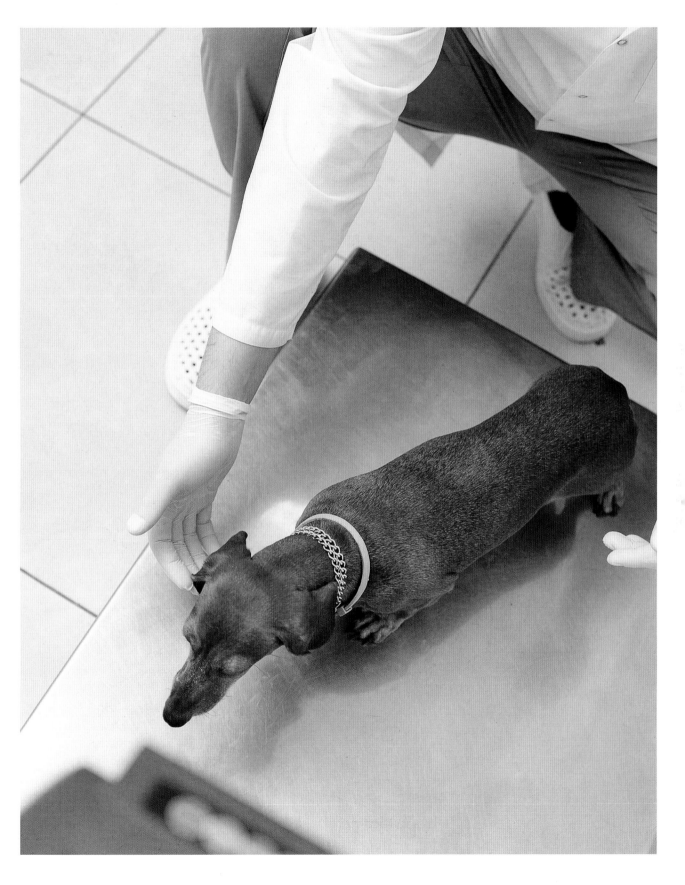

Sniffing and exploration

Dogs live in a world of scent, just as we live in a world of images. While we enjoy looking at people, at vistas, at the TV, dogs enjoy sniffing at scents left on the ground, at other dogs' faeces and bottoms, at the air as it wafts past them. We know that dogs' noses and the parts of their brain that detect scent are far superior to ours (see page 175). In comparison, our eyes see things in more detail and more vibrantly. Given how pleasurable and educational watching is for us, we can only assume that sniffing is the same for dogs.

With this in mind, giving your dog opportunities for sniffing is a great way to provide them with mental activity, in the same way as reading a book is for us. While we might take ourselves to the cinema when we want some fun, we can take our dogs somewhere new where there are plenty of interesting smells.

We have already discussed hide and seek games that you can play with your dog (see page 174). These are both physically and mentally stimulating. In a similar way, allowing your dog to run free in an area where other dogs or animals have been, letting them follow trails and investigate, and investigate places where they may have toileted or walked, seems to give them tremendous pleasure and you will find they spend a lot of time doing it. This is why it is a good idea to teach a recall so you can let your dog off lead to get on with this. Having a dog that keeps stopping to investigate while on the lead it incredibly tedious for us and we are likely to try to hurry them or pull them away. Giving your dog the time to do all the investigating they want is more satisfying for them and they will return home tired and more fulfilled.

Dogs seem to enjoy sniffing most smells, even ones we would find distasteful, but one type of smell seems to be more exciting than most and that is the trails of prey animals or birds that may have passed that way a long time ago. You will often see dogs, nose to the ground, weaving this way and that as they follow a trail, their tail up and helicoptering in a circular movement with the excitement.

Dogs can follow a scent trail for a long time and can be very dedicated to the task, even if they almost never find something at the end of it. This is because it feels good to stimulate the parts of the brain involved with 'seeking', in the same way that eating and other actions that keep us healthy give us a rewarding feeling[4,5]. Tracking prey probably gives dogs a similar feeling to the buzz we feel when we go to the shops to buy something special or at the start of a creative project where you are going to make something you will value. It is not just the end point that is enjoyable but all the intermediate parts too, which is why you may see your dog really enjoying tracking scent trails, even though the animal or bird is long gone. Indeed, sniffer dogs trained to search out drugs or explosives will work hard for many hours with just the reward of a game with a ball at the end. They are not only working for the game at the end but are likely to be enjoying all the seeking behaviour that goes into a successful detection.

Hunting

Hunting behaviour is natural and instinctive in most dogs, but often unacceptable to most pet dog owners, whether it's chasing squirrels in the park, chasing livestock in a field or running off after a deer or rabbit. Playing with toys can be a good substitute (see page 168) and it is possible to channel all your dog's hunting behaviour into games if they learn to play with toys instead from an early age. Hunting is such a natural activity, dogs find it very stimulating and satisfying and it provides both physical and mental exercise. This is why playing with toys can be so fulfilling for those dogs and owners that know how to play in a way that allows the dog to exercise all its natural innate hunting skills and instincts.

Play with other dogs

If your dog is sociable with other dogs, play sessions can use a great deal of mental energy. This can be spontaneously with other dogs you meet on a walk, dogs you arrange specific play dates with or your dog may have other dogs or a littermate that it lives with.

While play with other dogs can provide plenty of mental stimulation, there can be risks. Too much play with other dogs can put all the emphasis for daily pleasure onto other dogs resulting in a weaker bond and less of an interest in the people in your dog's life. This is particularly true of a puppy who may grow up playing with other dogs to the exclusion of its owners and this can have a detrimental effect on training to the point where they learn to ignore cues and run after other dogs instead. (See page 162.)

If your dog is well socialized with other dogs and plays well with them, successful play can enhance their lives, use up excess energy and be great fun for your dog. The amount of play with other dogs should always be balanced with plenty of games, training and interaction with humans however, so that they remain more responsive to you than to other dogs.

Mental activity is tiring

An energetic dog is often ready for more exercise, even after a long walk, but mental activity for the same amount of time, in the form of games with toys, hide and seek and training, seems to tire them much more and they are often ready for a good sleep afterwards (a repertoire of these activities can also be useful if your dog is injured and so cannot be exercised physically for a while). Including your dog in as many parts of your life as possible, with interesting outings and new places to explore, as well as giving plenty of opportunities for mental enrichment will result in a calm, contented dog.

The Natural Dog

In conclusion, all dogs need an owner who is able to provide for their needs, but lucky dogs have owners who put in just a bit more thought and effort to arrange for them to live their best life possible.

To take a holistic or wellness approach to dog care, owners need to find ways to achieve optimal physical and mental health for their dog. Good nutrition is the cornerstone to physical health, as is staying fit and combating diseases early with preventative measures. Spending quality time with your dog, being positive and loving, having fun and learning together, as well as keeping your dog busy and safe so they live without stress, are all essential for their mental health and, in turn, an ideal existence.

As with humans, a dog that is able to live optimally has a better chance of a happy, long life.

Providing ideal conditions for your dog is not necessarily about spending more money, but, instead, about making a bigger effort and probably giving a bit more time. The rewards are boundless, both for your dog and for your own peace of mind. Your relationship will flourish in a way that will make both of you happier, and your dog will be more content and well behaved. Knowing that you created a situation where your beloved dog had the happiest, longest life possible is priceless.

ENDNOTES

PART 1

CHAPTER 2

1. Day, M. J., Horzinek, M. C., Schultz, R. D., & Squires, R. A. 'WSAVA Guidelines for the vaccination of dogs and cats', *Journal of Small Animal Practice*, *57*(1), E1–E45, (2016). https://doi.org/10.1111/jsap.2_12431

2. Duval, D., & Giger, U. 'Vaccine-Associated Immune-Mediated Hemolytic Anemia in the Dog', *Journal of Veterinary Internal Medicine*, *10*(5), 290–295 (1996). https://doi.org/10.1111/j.1939-1676.1996.tb02064.x

3. Day, M. J., Horzinek, M. C., Schultz, R. D., & Squires, R. A. 'WSAVA Guidelines for the vaccination of dogs and cats', *Journal of Small Animal Practice*, *57*(1), E1–E45 (2016). https://doi.org/10.1111/jsap.2_12431

4. Lees, P., Pelligand, L., Whiting, M., Chambers, D., Toutain, P. L., & Whitehead, M. L. 'Comparison of veterinary drugs and veterinary homeopathy: part 2', *The Veterinary Record*, *181*(8), 198–207 (2017). https://doi.org/10.1136/vr.104279

5. *Clinical evidence for homeopathy*. (n.d.). Retrieved from https://www.england.nhs.uk/wp-content/uploads/2017/11/sps-homeopathy.pdf

CHAPTER 3

1. Deng, P., & Swanson, K. S. 'Gut microbiota of humans, dogs and cats: current knowledge and future opportunities and challenges', *British Journal of Nutrition*, *113*(S1), S6–S17 (2014). https://doi.org/10.1017/s0007114514002943

2. Xu, Z., & Knight, R. 'Dietary effects on human gut microbiome diversity', *British Journal of Nutrition*, *113*(S1), S1–S5 (2014). https://doi.org/10.1017/s0007114514004127

3. Valdes, A. M., Walter, J., Segal, E., & Spector, T. D. 'Role of the gut microbiota in nutrition and health', *BMJ*, k2179 (2018). https://doi.org/10.1136/bmj.k2179

4. Xu, Z., & Knight, R. 'Dietary effects on human gut microbi-
ome diversity', *British Journal of Nutrition*, *113*(S1), S1–S5 (2014). https://doi.org/10.1017/s0007114514004127

5. Sandri, M., Dal Monego, S., Conte, G., Sgorlon, S., & Stefanon, B. 'Raw meat based diet influences faecal microbiome and end products of fermentation in healthy dogs', *BMC Veterinary Research*, *13*(1) (2016). https://doi.org/10.1186/s12917-017-0981-z

6. Bosch, G., Hagen-Plantinga, E. A., & Hendriks, W. H. 'Dietary nutrient profiles of wild wolves: insights for optimal dog nutrition?', *British Journal of Nutrition*, *113*(S1), S40–S54 (2015). https://doi.org/10.1017/S0007114514002311

7. Chapman, C. M. C., Gibson, G. R., & Rowland, I. 'Health benefits of probiotics: are mixtures more effective than single strains?', *European Journal of Nutrition*, *50*(1), 1–17 (2011). https://doi.org/10.1007/s00394-010-0166-z

8. Hendriks, W. H., Tran, Q. D., van der Poel, A. F. B. 'Effects of extrusion processing on nutrients in dry pet food', *Journal of the Science of Food and Agriculture, Mini-review (2008)*. https://onlinelibrary.wiley.com/journal/10970010

9. Kahl, R., Kappus, H. 'Toxicology of the synthetic antioxidants BHA and BHT in comparison with the natural antioxidant vitamin E', University of Hamburg (1993). https://www.ncbi.nlm.nih.gov/pubmed/8493816

10. 'Butylated Hydroxyanisole', *Report on Carcinogens, Fourteenth Edition, National Toxicity Program, U.S. Department of Health and Human Studies (2016)*. https://ntp.niehs.nih.gov/ntp/roc/content/profiles/butylatedhydroxyanisole.pdf

11. 'The effect of butylated hydroxyanisole and butylated hydroxytoluene on behavioral development of mice', Loyola University, Illinois (1974). http://www.feingold.org/Research/stokes.html

12. Commission Implementing Regulation (EU) 2017/962 (2017). https://eur-lex.europa.eu/legal-content/EN/TXT/PDF/?uri=CELEX:32017R0962&from=EN

13. Bateman, B. 'The effects of a double blind, placebo controlled,

artificial food colourings and benzoate preservative challenge on hyperactivity in a general population sample of preschool children', *Archives of Disease in Childhood, 89*(6), 506–511 (2004). https://doi.org/10.1136/adc.2003.031435

14. Neitz, J., Geist, T., & Jacobs, G. H. 'Color vision in the dog', *Visual Neuroscience, 3*(2), 119–125 (1989). https://doi.org/10.1017/s0952523800004430

15. Jacobs, G. H., Deegan, J. F., Crognale, M. A., & Fenwick, J. A. 'Photopigments of dogs and foxes and their implications for canid vision', *Visual Neuroscience, 10*(1), 173–180 (1993). https://doi.org/10.1017/s0952523800003291

16. Axelsson, E., Ratnakumar, A., Arendt, M.-L., Maqbool, K., Webster, M. T., Perloski, M., …Lindblad-Toh, K. 'The genomic signature of dog domestication reveals adaptation to a starch-rich diet', *Nature, 495*(7441), 360–364 (2013). https://doi.org/10.1038/nature11837

17. 'Study finds overweight dogs live shorter lives' (n.d.). Retrieved from https://www.avma.org/News/JAVMANews/Pages/190301n.aspx

18. Yano, J. M., Yu, K., Donaldson, G. P., Shastri, G. G., Ann, P., Ma, L., …Hsiao, E. Y. 'Indigenous bacteria from the gut microbiota regulate host serotonin biosynthesis', *Cell, 161*(2), 264–276 (2015). https://doi.org/10.1016/j.cell.2015.02.047

19. Jenkins, T., Nguyen, J., Polglaze, K., & Bertrand, P. 'Influence of tryptophan and serotonin on mood and cognition with a possible role of the gut-brain axis', *Nutrients, 8*(1), 56 (2016). https://doi.org/10.3390/nu8010056

20. Roberts, M. T., Bermingham, E. N., Cave, N. J., Young, W., McKenzie, C. M., & Thomas, D. G. 'Macronutrient intake of dogs, self-selecting diets varying in composition offered ad libitum', *Journal of Animal Physiology and Animal Nutrition, 102*(2), 568–575 (2017). https://doi.org/10.1111/jpn.12794

21. Bosch, G., Hagen-Plantinga, E. A., & Hendriks, W. H. 'Dietary nutrient profiles of wild wolves: insights for optimal dog nutrition?', *British Journal of Nutrition, 113*(S1), S40–S54 (2015). https://doi.org/10.1017/S0007114514002311

22. Nutritional Effects of Food Processing – NutritionData.com. (2016). Retrieved from https://nutritiondata.self.com/topics/processing

23. Sandberg, M., Hofshagen, M., Østensvik, Ø., Skjerve, E., & Innocent, G. 'Survival of Campylobacter on frozen broiler carcasses as a function of time', *Journal of Food Protection, 68*(8), 1600–1605 (2005). https://doi.org/10.4315/0362-028x-68.8.1600

24. Georgsson, F., Þorkelsson, Á. E., Geirsdóttir, M., Reiersen, J., & Stern, N. J. 'The influence of freezing and duration of storage on Campylobacter and indicator bacteria in broiler carcasses', *Food Microbiology, 23*(7), 677–683 (2006). https://doi.org/10.1016/j.fm.2005.10.003

25. M. Mesías, F. Holgado, R. Sevenich, J. Briand, Gloria Márquez Ruiz, & F. Morales 'Fatty acids profile in canned tuna and sardine after retort sterilization and high pressure thermal sterilization treatment' (2015). Retrieved from https://www.semanticscholar.org/paper/Fatty-acids-profile-in-canned-tuna-and-sardine-and-Mes%C3%ADas-Holgado/eb923717fb435fd65a0dddd1e20e4d-e59a527081

26. Brown, S. (2010) *Unlocking the Canine Ancestral Diet : Healthier Dog the ABC Way*. Washington: Dogwise Publishing

27. Brown, S. (2010) *Unlocking the Canine Ancestral Diet : Healthier Dog the ABC Way*. Washington: Dogwise Publishing

28. Kealy, R. D., Lawler, D. F., Ballam, J. M., Mantz, S. L., Biery, D. N., Greeley, E. H., …Stowe, H. D. 'Effects of diet restriction on life span and age-related changes in dogs', *Journal of the American Veterinary Medical Association, 220*(9), 1315–1320 (2002). https://doi.org/10.2460/javma.2002.220.1315

29. Salt, C., Morris, P. J., Wilson, D., Lund, E. M., & German, A. J. 'Association between life span and body condition in neutered client-owned dogs', *Journal of Veterinary Internal Medicine* (2018). https://doi.org/10.1111/jvim.15367

30. Yam, P. S., Butowski, C. F., Chitty, J. L., Naughton, G., Wiseman-Orr, M. L., Parkin, T., & Reid, J. 'Impact of canine overweight and obesity on health-related quality of life', *Preventive Veterinary Medicine, 127*, 64–69 (2016). https://doi.org/10.1016/j.prevetmed.2016.03.013

31. German, A. J., Ryan, V. H., German, A. C., Wood, I. S., & Trayhurn, P. 'Obesity, its associated disorders and the role of inflammatory adipokines in companion animals', *The Veterinary Journal, 185*(1), 4–9 (2010). https://doi.org/10.1016/j.tvjl.2010.04.004

32. German, A. J., Hervera, M., Hunter, L., Holden, S. L., Morris,

P. J., Biourge, V., & Trayhurn, P. 'Improvement in insulin resistance and reduction in plasma inflammatory adipokines after weight loss in obese dogs', *Domestic Animal Endocrinology*, *37*(4), 214–226 (2009). https://doi.org/10.1016/j.domaniend.2009.07.001

33. Tvarijonaviciute, A., Ceron, J. J., Holden, S. L., Cuthbertson, D. J., Biourge, V., Morris, P. J., & German, A. J. 'Obesity-related metabolic dysfunction in dogs: a comparison with human metabolic syndrome', *BMC Veterinary Research*, *8*(1), 147 (2012). https://doi.org/10.1186/1746-6148-8-147

34. 'Diet restriction and ageing in the dog: major observations over two decades – CORRIGENDUM', *British Journal of Nutrition*, *101*(7), 1112–1112 (2008). https://doi.org/10.1017/s0007114508050265

35. Lindhe, J., Hamp, S. E., & Loe, H. 'Plaque induced periodontal disease in beagle dogs', *Journal of Periodontal Research*, *10*(5), 243–255 (1975). https://doi.org/10.1111/j.1600-0765.1975.tb00031.x

36. Hayes, G. 'Gastrointestinal foreign bodies in dogs and cats: a retrospective study of 208 cases', *Journal of Small Animal Practice*, *50*(11), 576–583 (2009). https://doi.org/10.1111/j.1748-5827.2009.00783.x

37. Marx, F., Machado, G., Pezzali, J., Marcolla, C., Kessler, A., Ahlstrøm, Ø., & Trevizan, L. 'Raw beef bones as chewing items to reduce dental calculus in Beagle dogs', *Australian Veterinary Journal*, *94*(1–2), 18–23 (2016). https://doi.org/10.1111/avj.12394

CHAPTER 4

1. Horowitz, A. (2016) *Being a Dog: Following the Dog into a World of Smell*, Simon & Schuster

CHAPTER 5

1. Ni a ski, W., Levy, X., Ochota, M., & Pasikowska, J. 'Pharmacological Treatment for Common Prostatic Conditions in Dogs – Benign Prostatic Hyperplasia and Prostatitis: an Update', *Reproduction in Domestic Animals*, *49*, 8–15 (2014). https://doi.org/10.1111/rda.12297

2. Smith, A. N. 'The Role of Neutering in Cancer Development', *Veterinary Clinics of North America: Small Animal Practice*, *44*(5), 965–975 (2014). https://doi.org/10.1016/j.cvsm.2014.06.003

3. Kustritz, M. V. R. 'Determining the optimal age for gonadectomy of dogs and cats', *Journal of the American Veterinary Medical Association*, *231*(11), 1665–1675 (2007). https://doi.org/10.2460/javma.231.11.1665

4. Liao, A. T., Chu, P. Y., Yeh, L. S., Lin, C. T., & Liu, C. H. 'A 12-Year Retrospective Study of Canine Testicular Tumors', *Journal of Veterinary Medical Science*, *71*(7), 919–923 (2009). https://doi.org/10.1292/jvms.71.919

5. Aaron, A., Eggleton, K., Power, C., & Holt, P. E. 'Urethral sphincter mechanism incompetence in male dogs: a retrospective analysis of 54 cases', *Veterinary Record*, *139*(22), 542–546 (1996). https://doi.org/10.1136/vr.139.22.542

6. Salmeri, K. R., Bloomberg, M. S., Scruggs, S. L., & Shille, V. 'Gonadectomy in immature dogs: effects on skeletal, physical, and behavioral development', *Journal of the American Veterinary Medical Association*, *198*(7), 1193–1203 (1991). Retrieved from https://pubmed.ncbi.nlm.nih.gov/2045340/

7. Spain, C. V., Scarlett, J. M., & Houpt, K. A. 'Long-term risks and benefits of early-age gonadectomy in dogs', *Journal of the American Veterinary Medical Association*, *224*(3), 380–387 (2004). https://doi.org/10.2460/javma.2004.224.380

8. Duerr, F. M., Duncan, C. G., Savicky, R. S., Park, R. D., Egger, E. L., & Palmer, R. H. 'Risk factors for excessive tibial plateau angle in large-breed dogs with cranial cruciate ligament disease', *Journal of the American Veterinary Medical Association*, *231*(11), 1688–1691 (2007). https://doi.org/10.2460/javma.231.11.1688

9. Torres de la Riva, G., Hart, B. L., Farver, T. B., Oberbauer, A. M., Messam, L. L. M., Willits, N., & Hart, L. A. 'Neutering Dogs: Effects on Joint Disorders and Cancers in Golden Retrievers', *PLoS ONE*, *8*(2), e55937 (2013). https://doi.org/10.1371/journal.pone.0055937

10. Hart, B. L., Hart, L. A., Thigpen, A. P., & Willits, N. H. 'Long-Term Health Effects of Neutering Dogs: Comparison of Labrador Retrievers with Golden Retrievers', *PLoS ONE*, *9*(7), e102241 (2014). https://doi.org/10.1371/journal.pone.0102241

11. Lefebvre, S. L., Yang, M., Wang, M., Elliott, D. A., Buff, P. R., & Lund, E. M. 'Effect of age at gonadectomy on the probability of dogs becoming overweight', *Journal of the American Veterinary Medical Association*, *243*(2), 236–243 (2013). https://doi.org/10.2460/javma.243.2.236

12. Torres de la Riva, G., Hart, B. L., Farver, T. B., Oberbauer, A. M., Messam, L. L. M., Willits, N., & Hart, L. A. 'Neutering Dogs: Effects on Joint Disorders and Cancers in Golden Retrievers', *PLoS ONE*, *8*(2), e55937 (2013). https://doi.org/10.1371/journal.pone.0055937

13. Zink, M. C., Farhoody, P., Elser, S. E., Ruffini, L. D., Gibbons, T. A., & Rieger, R. H. 'Evaluation of the risk and age of onset of cancer and behavioral disorders in gonadectomized Vizslas', *Journal of the American Veterinary Medical Association*, *244*(3), 309–319 (2014). https://doi.org/10.2460/javma.244.3.309

14 Norris, A. M., Laing, E. J., Valli, V. E. O., Withrow, S. J., Macy, D. W., Ogilvie, G. K., …Jacobs, R. M. 'Canine Bladder and Urethral Tumors: A Retrospective Study of 115 Cases (1980–1985)', *Journal of Veterinary Internal Medicine*, *6*(3), 145–153 (1992). https://doi.org/10.1111/j.1939-1676.1992.tb00330.x

15. Ware, W. A., & Hopper, D. L. 'Cardiac Tumors in Dogs: 1982–1995', *Journal of Veterinary Internal Medicine*, *13*(2), 95–103 (1999). https://doi.org/10.1111/j.1939-1676.1999.tb01136.x

16. Ru, G., Terracini, B., & Glickman, L. T. 'Host related risk factors for canine osteosarcoma', *The Veterinary Journal*, *156*(1), 31–39 (1998). https://doi.org/10.1016/s1090-0233(98)80059-2

17. Cooley, D. M., Beranek, B. C., Schlittler, D. L., Glickman, N. W., Glickman, L. T., & Waters, D. J. 'Endogenous gonadal hormone exposure and bone sarcoma risk', *Cancer Epidemiology, Biomarkers & Prevention: A Publication of the American Association for Cancer Research, 11*(11), 1434–1440 (2002). Retrieved from https://pubmed.ncbi.nlm.nih.gov/12433723/

18. Sundburg, C. R., Belanger, J. M., Bannasch, D. L., Famula, T. R., & Oberbauer, A. M. 'Gonadectomy effects on the risk of immune disorders in the dog: a retrospective study', *BMC Veterinary Research*, *12*(1) (2016). https://doi.org/10.1186/s12917-016-0911-5

19. Moore, G. E., Guptill, L. F., Ward, M. P., Glickman, N. W., Faunt, K. K., Lewis, H. B., & Glickman, L. T. 'Adverse events diagnosed within three days of vaccine administration in dogs', *Journal of the American Veterinary Medical Association*, *227*(7), 1102–1108 (2005). https://doi.org/10.2460/javma.2005.227.1102

20. Hart, B. L. 'Effect of gonadectomy on subsequent development of age-related cognitive impairment in dogs', *Journal of the American Veterinary Medical Association*, *219*(1), 51–56 (2001). https://doi.org/10.2460/javma.2001.219.51

21. Hagman, R. 'New aspects of canine pyometra' (2004). Retrieved from https://pub.epsilon.slu.se/736/

22. Schneider, R., Dorn, C. R. & Taylor, D. O., 'Factors influencing canine mammary cancer development and postsurgical survival', *Journal of the National Cancer Institute* 43, 1249–61 (1969). https://doi.org/10.1093/jnci/43.6.1249

23. Beauvais, W., Cardwell, J. M., & Brodbelt, D. C. 'The effect of neutering on the risk of mammary tumours in dogs – a systematic review', *The Journal of Small Animal Practice*, *53*(6), 314–322 (2012). https://doi.org/10.1111/j.1748-5827.2011.01220.x

24. Smith, A. N. 'The Role of Neutering in Cancer Development', *Veterinary Clinics of North America: Small Animal Practice*, *44*(5), 965–975 (2014). https://doi.org/10.1016/j.cvsm.2014.06.003

25. Thrusfield, M. V., Holt, P. E., & Muirhead, R. H. 'Acquired urinary incontinence in bitches: its incidence and relationship to neutering practices', *Journal of Small Animal Practice*, *39*(12), 559–566 (1998). https://doi.org/10.1111/j.1748-5827.1998.tb03709.x

26. Spain, C. V., Scarlett, J. M., & Houpt, K. A. 'Long-term risks and benefits of early-age gonadectomy in dogs', *Journal of the American Veterinary Medical Association*, *224*(3), 380–387 (2004). https://doi.org/10.2460/javma.2004.224.380

27. Stöcklin-Gautschi, N. M., Hässig, M., Reichler, I. M., Hubler, M., & Arnold, S. 'The relationship of urinary incontinence to early spaying in bitches', *Journal of Reproduction and Fertility*. Supplement, 57, 233–236 (2001). Retrieved from https://pubmed.ncbi.nlm.nih.gov/11787155/

28. Beauvais, W., Cardwell, J. M., & Brodbelt, D. C. 'The effect of neutering on the risk of urinary incontinence in bitches – a systematic review', *Journal of Small Animal Practice*, *53*(4), 198–204 (2012). https://doi.org/10.1111/j.1748-5827.2011.01176.x

29. Elliot, M., 'Neutering your dog – making an informed decision' (2016). Retrieved from https://www.wolftucker.co.uk/blog/neutering-your-dog-making-an-informed-decision/

30. Spain, C.V., Scarlett, J. M., & Houpt, K. A. 'Long-term risks and benefits of early-age gonadectomy in dogs', *Journal of the American Veterinary Medical Association*, *224*(3), 380–387 (2004). https://doi.org/10.2460/javma.2004.224.380

31. Salmeri, K. R., Bloomberg, M. S., Scruggs, S. L., & Shille, V. 'Gonadectomy in immature dogs: effects on skeletal, physical, and behavioral development', *Journal of the American Veterinary Medical Association*, *198*(7), 1193–1203 (1991). Retrieved from https://pubmed.ncbi.nlm.nih.gov/2045340/

32. Duerr, F. M., Duncan, C. G., Savicky, R. S., Park, R. D., Egger, E. L., & Palmer, R. H. 'Risk factors for excessive tibial plateau angle in large-breed dogs with cranial cruciate ligament disease', *Journal of the American Veterinary Medical Association*, *231*(11), 1688–1691 (2007). https://doi.org/10.2460/javma.231.11.1688

33. Hart, B. L., Hart, L. A., Thigpen, A. P., & Willits, N. H. 'Long-term health effects of neutering dogs: comparison of labrador retrievers with golden retrievers', *PLoS ONE*, *9*(7), e102241 (2014). https://doi.org/10.1371/journal.pone.0102241

34. Howe, L. M., Slater, M. R., Boothe, H. W., Hobson, H. P., Holcom, J. L., & Spann, A. C. 'Long-term outcome of gonadectomy performed at an early age or traditional age in dogs', *Journal of the American Veterinary Medical Association*, *218*(2), 217–221 (2001). https://doi.org/10.2460/javma.2001.218.217

35. Torres de la Riva, G., Hart, B. L., Farver, T. B., Oberbauer, A. M., Messam, L. L. M., Willits, N., & Hart, L. A. 'Neutering dogs: effects on joint disorders and cancers in golden retrievers', *PLoS ONE*, *8*(2), e55937 (2013). https://doi.org/10.1371/journal.pone.0055937

36. Spain, C.V., Scarlett, J. M., & Houpt, K. A. 'Long-term risks and benefits of early-age gonadectomy in dogs', *Journal of the American Veterinary Medical Association*, *224*(3), 380–387 (2004). https://doi.org/10.2460/javma.2004.224.380

37. Lefebvre, S. L., Yang, M., Wang, M., Elliott, D. A., Buff, P. R., & Lund, E. M. 'Effect of age at gonadectomy on the probability of dogs becoming overweight', *Journal of the American Veterinary Medical Association*, *243*(2), 236–243 (2013). https://doi.org/10.2460/javma.243.2.236

38. Spain, C.V., Scarlett, J. M., & Houpt, K. A. 'Long-term risks and benefits of early-age gonadectomy in dogs', *Journal of the American Veterinary Medical Association*, *224*(3), 380–387 (2004).

https://doi.org/10.2460/javma.2004.224.380

39. Villamil, J. A., Henry, C. J., Hahn, A. W., Bryan, J. N., Tyler, J. W., & Caldwell, C. W. 'Hormonal and sex impact on the epidemiology of canine lymphoma', *Journal of Cancer Epidemiology*, 1–7 (2009). https://doi.org/10.1155/2009/591753

40. Norris, A. M., Laing, E. J., Valli, V. E. O., Withrow, S. J., Macy, D. W., Ogilvie, G. K., …Jacobs, R. M. 'Canine bladder and urethral tumors: a retrospective study of 115 cases (1980–1985)', *Journal of Veterinary Internal Medicine*, *6*(3), 145–153 (1992). https://doi.org/10.1111/j.1939-1676.1992.tb00330.x

41. Torres de la Riva, G., Hart, B. L., Farver, T. B., Oberbauer, A. M., Messam, L. L. M., Willits, N., & Hart, L. A. 'Neutering dogs: effects on joint disorders and cancers in golden retrievers', *PLoS ONE*, *8*(2), e55937 (2013). https://doi.org/10.1371/journal.pone.0055937

42. Zink, M. C., Farhoody, P., Elser, S. E., Ruffini, L. D., Gibbons, T. A., & Rieger, R. H. 'Evaluation of the risk and age of onset of cancer and behavioral disorders in gonadectomized Vizslas', *Journal of the American Veterinary Medical Association*, *244*(3), 309–319 (2014). https://doi.org/10.2460/javma.244.3.309

43. Prymak, C., McKee, L. J., Goldschmidt, M. H., & Glickman, L. T. 'Epidemiologic, clinical, pathologic, and prognostic characteristics of splenic hemangiosarcoma and splenic hematoma in dogs: 217 cases (1985)', *Journal of the American Veterinary Medical Association*, *193*(6), 706–712 (1988). Retrieved from https://pubmed.ncbi.nlm.nih.gov/3192450/

44. Ware, W. A., & Hopper, D. L. 'Cardiac tumors in dogs: 1982–1995', *Journal of Veterinary Internal Medicine*, *13*(2), 95–103 (1999). https://doi.org/10.1111/j.1939-1676.1999.tb01136.x

45. Ru, G., Terracini, B., & Glickman, L. T. 'Host related risk factors for canine osteosarcoma', *The Veterinary Journal*, *156*(1), 31–39 (1998). https://doi.org/10.1016/s1090-0233(98)80059-2

46. Cooley, D. M., Beranek, B. C., Schlittler, D. L., Glickman, N. W., Glickman, L. T., & Waters, D. J. 'Endogenous gonadal hormone exposure and bone sarcoma risk', *Cancer Epidemiology, Biomarkers & Prevention: A Publication of the American Association for Cancer Research, 11*(11), 1434–1440 (2002). Retrieved from https://pubmed.ncbi.nlm.nih.gov/12433723/

47. Azkona, G., García-Belenguer, S., Chacón, G., Rosado, B.,

León, M., & Palacio, J. 'Prevalence and risk factors of behavioural changes associated with age-related cognitive impairment in geriatric dogs', *Journal of Small Animal Practice*, *50*(2), 87–91 (2009). https://doi.org/10.1111/j.1748-5827.2008.00718.x

48. Sundburg, C. R., Belanger, J. M., Bannasch, D. L., Famula, T. R., & Oberbauer, A. M. 'Gonadectomy effects on the risk of immune disorders in the dog: a retrospective study', *BMC Veterinary Research*, *12*(1) (2016). https://doi.org/10.1186/s12917-016-0911-5

49. Moore, G. E., Guptill, L. F., Ward, M. P., Glickman, N. W., Faunt, K. K., Lewis, H. B., & Glickman, L. T. 'Adverse events diagnosed within three days of vaccine administration in dogs', *Journal of the American Veterinary Medical Association*, *227*(7), 1102–1108 (2005). https://doi.org/10.2460/javma.2005.227.1102

50. Kaufmann, C. A., Forndran, S., Stauber, C., Woerner, K., & Gansloßer, U. 'The social behaviour of neutered male dogs compared to intact dogs (Canis lupus familiaris): video analyses, questionnaires and case studies', *Veterinary Medicine – Open Journal*, *2*(1), 22–37 (2017). https://doi.org/10.17140/vmoj-2-113

CHAPTER 6
1. Handlin, L., Hydbring-Sandberg, E., Nilsson, A., Ejdebäck, M., Jansson, A., & Uvnäs-Moberg, K. 'Short-term interaction between dogs and their owners: effects on oxytocin, cortisol, insulin and heart rate – an exploratory study', *Anthrozoös*, *24*(3), 301–315 (2011). https://doi.org/10.2752/175303711x13045914865385

2. Sapolsky, R. M. (2004) *Why Zebras Don't Get Ulcers: The Acclaimed Guide to Stress, Stress-Related Diseases, and Coping*. New York: St Martin's Press

PART 2

CHAPTER 1
1. Tierney, J. (2020) *The Power of Bad: And How to Overcome It*. London: Penguin Books Ltd

2. Gottman, J. M., Coan, J., Carrere, S., & Swanson, C. 'Predicting marital happiness and stability from newlywed interactions', *Journal of Marriage and the Family*, *60*(1), 5 (1998). https://doi.org/10.2307/353438

CHAPTER 2
1. Bonanni, R., Cafazzo, S., Abis, A., Barillari, E., Valsecchi, P., & Natoli, E. 'Age-graded dominance hierarchies and social tolerance in packs of free-ranging dogs', *Behavioral Ecology*, *28*(4), 1004–1020 (2017). ttps://doi.org/10.1093/beheco/arx059

CHAPTER 3
1. Cirelli, C., & Tononi, G. 'Is sleep essential?', *PLoS Biology*, *6*(8), e216 (2008). https://doi.org/10.1371/journal.pbio.0060216

2. Irwin, M., McClintick, J., Costlow, C., Fortner, M., White, J., & Gillin, J. C. 'Partial night sleep deprivation reduces natural killer and cellular immune responses in humans', *The FASEB Journal*, *10*(5), 643–653 (1996). https://doi.org/10.1096/fasebj.10.5.8621064

3. Boonstra, T. W., Stins, J. F., Daffertshofer, A., & Beek, P. J. 'Effects of sleep deprivation on neural functioning: an integrative review', *Cellular and Molecular Life Sciences*, *64*(7–8), 934–946 (2007). https://doi.org/10.1007/s00018-007-6457-8

4. Lucas, E. A., Powell, E. W., & Murphree, O. D. 'Baseline sleep-wake patterns in the pointer dog', *Physiology & Behavior*, *19*(2), 285–291 (1977). https://doi.org/10.1016/0031-9384(77)90340-7

5. Adams, G. J., & Johnson, K. G. 'Sleep-wake cycles and other night-time behaviours of the domestic dog Canis familiaris', *Applied Animal Behaviour Science*, *36*(2–3), 233–248 (1993). https://doi.org/10.1016/0168-1591(93)90013-f

6. Amis, T. C., & Kurpershoek, C. 'Pattern of breathing in brachycephalic dogs', *American Journal of Veterinary Research*, *47*(10), 2200–2204 (1986). Retrieved from https://pubmed.ncbi.nlm.nih.gov/3777646/

7. Hendricks, J. C., Kline, L. R., Kovalski, R. J., O'Brien, J. A., Morrison, A. R., & Pack, A. I. 'The English bulldog: a natural model of sleep-disordered breathing', *Journal of Applied Physiology*, *63*(4), 1344–1350 (1987). https://doi.org/10.1152/jappl.1987.63.4.1344

8. Neilson, J. C., Hart, B. L., Cliff, K. D., & Ruehl, W. W. 'Prevalence of behavioral changes associated with age-related cognitive impairment in dogs', *Journal of the American Veterinary Medical Association*, *218*(11), 1787–1791 (2001). https://doi.org/10.2460/javma.2001.218.1787

9. Rofina, J. E., van Ederen, A. M., Toussaint, M. J. M., Secrève, M., van der Spek, A., van der Meer, I., …Gruys, E. 'Cognitive disturbances in old dogs suffering from the canine counterpart of Alzheimer's disease', *Brain Research*, *1069*(1), 216–226 (2006). https://doi.org/10.1016/j.brainres.2005.11.021

10. Headey, B., Na, F., & Zheng, R. 'Pet dogs benefit owners' health: a 'natural experiment' in China', *Social Indicators Research*, *87*(3), 481–493 (2007). https://doi.org/10.1007/s11205-007-9142-2

11. Adams, G. J., & Johnson, K. G. 'Behavioural responses to barking and other auditory stimuli during night-time sleeping and waking in the domestic dog (Canis familiaris)', *Applied Animal Behaviour Science*, *39*(2), 151–162 (1994). https://doi.org/10.1016/0168-1591(94)90135-x

CHAPTER 4

1 Bekoff. M. & Byers. J. A., (1998) *Animal Play, Cambridge University Press*

2. Walker, J. C. 'Human odor detectability: new methodology used to determine threshold and variation', *Chemical Senses*, *28*(9), 817–826 (2003). https://doi.org/10.1093/chemse/bjg075

3. Walker, D. B., Walker, J. C., Cavnar, P. J., Taylor, J. L., Pickel, D. H., Hall, S. B., & Suarez, J. C. 'Naturalistic quantification of canine olfactory sensitivity', *Applied Animal Behaviour Science*, *97*(2–4), 241–254 (2006). https://doi.org/10.1016/j.applanim.2005.07.009

4. Craven, B. A., Paterson, E. G., & Settles, G. S. 'The fluid dynamics of canine olfaction: unique nasal airflow patterns as an explanation of macrosmia', *Journal of The Royal Society Interface*, *7*(47), 933–943 (2009). https://doi.org/10.1098/rsif.2009.0490

5. Horowitz, A. (2016) *Being a Dog: Following the Dog into a World of Smell, Simon & Schuster*

CHAPTER 5

1. Rodrigues, S. M., LeDoux, J. E., & Sapolsky, R. M. 'The influence of stress hormones on fear circuitry', *Annual Review of Neuroscience*, *32*(1), 289–313 (2009). https://doi.org/10.1146/annurev.neuro.051508.135620

2. Appleby, D. L., Bradshaw, J. W. S., & Casey, R. A. 'Relationship between aggressive and avoidance behaviour by dogs and their experience in the first six months of life', *Veterinary Record*, *150*(14), 434–438 (2002). https://doi.org/10.1136/vr.150.14.434

3. Sapolsky, R. M. (2004) *Why Zebras Don't Get Ulcers: The Acclaimed Guide to Stress, Stress-Related Diseases, and Coping. New York: St Martin's Press*

4. Sundman, A. S., Van Poucke, E., Svensson Holm, A. C., Faresjö, Å., Theodorsson, E., Jensen, P., & Roth, L. S. V. 'Long-term stress levels are synchronized in dogs and their owners', *Scientific Reports*, *9*(1) (2019). https://doi.org/10.1038/s41598-019-43851-x

5. Tierney, J. (2020) *The Power of Bad: And How to Overcome It. London: Penguin Books Ltd*

6. Hart, B., & Risley, T. (1995) *Meaningful Differences in Everyday Experience of Young American Children, Baltimore: H. Brookes*

7. Gottman, J. M., Coan, J., Carrere, S., & Swanson, C. 'Predicting marital happiness and stability from newlywed interactions', *Journal of Marriage and the Family*, *60*(1), 5 (1998). https://doi.org/10.2307/353438

CHAPTER 6

1. Tierney, J. (2020) *The Power of Bad: And How to Overcome It. London: Penguin Books Ltd*

2. Hart, B., & Risley, T. (1995) *Meaningful Differences in Everyday Experience of Young American Children, Baltimore: H. Brookes*

3. Gottman, J. M., Coan, J., Carrere, S., & Swanson, C. 'Predicting marital happiness and stability from newlywed interactions', *Journal of Marriage and the Family*, *60*(1), 5 (1998). https://doi.org/10.2307/353438

4. Pryor, K. (2010) *Reaching the Animal Mind: Clicker Training and What It Teaches Us about All Animals, Scribner Book Company*

5. Panksepp, J. (2004) Affective Neuroscience: The Foundations of Human and Animal Emotions, Oxford University Press

All websites accessed February 2020

INDEX

PICTURE CREDITS

123RF Alexey Antipov 34; annaav 2; brusnik 10; lightfieldstudios 88, 177; luckybusiness 115; tan4iKK 146.

age fotostock Juniors Bildarchive 24.

Alamy Stock Photo Andrew Wilson 101; Ashley Western 99; Charlotte Banfield 32; Farlap 14; pedphoto36pm 60; Penny Koukoulas 96; Petra Wegner 94; Tierfotoagentur/J. Hutfluss 55; Tierfotoagentur/M. Rohlf 58; Tierfotoagentur/R. Richter 185.

Gwen Bailey 6, 195, 204.

Dreamstime.com Bazuzzza 57, 59; Evgeniy Kalinovskiy 203; Kairi Aun 51; Otsphoto 119.

Getty Images Chris Winsor 156; Westend61 122.

iStock alexei_tm 48, 118, 129, 191, 206; AnnaStills 154; betyarlaca 83; Bigandt_Photography 12; bymuratdeniz 114; Capuski 65, 120, 183; CBCK-Christine 172; cunfek 159; dageldog 4, 16, 26, 76, 134, 164, 168; damedeeso 130; Daniel Besic 149; dexter_s 112; DGLimages 132; diego_cervo 140; DieterMeyrl 93; ela bracho 126; Extreme-Photographer 192; fcscafeine 9; Fertographer 25; fotoVoyager 208; fotyma 207; FreshSplash 75; gabrielabertolini 66; GeorgePeters 178; Georgijevic 187; gollykim 33, 151; Groomee 200; hnijjar007 199; image_ jungle 52; jodie777 161; K_Thalhofer 163, 174, 198; Ksenia Raykova 44; LuPa Creative 145; M. Kaercher 171; Magdanphoto 45; Marcus Lindstrom 18; Matt Francis 28, 30; mediaphotos 117; mis1il 42; monkeybusinessimages 136; Nastasic 107; Nevena1987 133; nycshooter 160; O_Lypa 108; olgagorovenko 70; Orbon Alija 21; ozgurdonmaz 142; Pekic 15; Ryan Hoel 102; RyanJLane 124; sdominick 152; shellhawker 224; shironosov 139; skynesher 109; Solovyova 22; SolStock 104, 210; Sonja Rachbauer 106; timnewman 181; Vasyl Dolmatov 111; vauvau 182; Viorel Kurnosov 81; wundervisuals 144; Ziga Plahutar 188.

Raw Pet Foods (rawpetfoods.co.uk) 64.

Shutterstock all_about_people 39; Ammit Jack 36; Atip Kantajai 40; buchsammy 90; Darisha Design 68; dezy 38; ESB Professional 62; Estelle R 87; Flatka 197; FotoSimko 46; Jarun Ontakrai 56; Jean Doyon 186; kiyechka53 184; Oleksiy Rezin 155; schubbel 85; Teera Pittayanurak 79; unguryanu 166.

Unsplash Jacob Curtis 125; Oscar Sutton 19.

WSAVA 78.

ACKNOWLEDGEMENTS

I would like to thank my publisher, Trevor Davies, whose vision of this book contained a lot more on the health aspects of dogs than I was initially willing to write. I was lucky enough to secure a brave and brilliant holistic veterinary surgeon, Nick Thompson, who helped fill in the gaps in my knowledge and enabled me to write a more balanced book than would otherwise have been possible.

I have been fortunate to learn my behaviour knowledge from the most eminent dog behavourists and trainers and I would like to thank them all for being willing to share their wisdom and for all they have taught me. In addition, I have learnt from many dogs throughout my pioneering work in rescue shelters so long ago and I am grateful to them all and sorry for those who I didn't have quite enough knowledge to help at the time. The rescue dogs and puppies that have shared my life have brought a greater clarity of understanding and I am grateful to all for their love and their generous and willing natures.

My acknowledgements would not be complete without a mention for those hard at work at the publishers who edited and designed this book with great skill and creativity.